W9-BBW-801

One Word, Two Words, Hyphen- ated?

MARY LOUISE GILMAN

Gilman, Mary Louise.
    One word, two words, hyphenated? / Mary Louise Gilman.
        p.   cm.
    Includes bibliographical references (p. iii).
    ISBN 1-881859-01-0 (pbk.)
        1. Spellers. 2. English language -- Terms and phrases.   I. Title.
PE1146.G56 1998   97-39429
423'.1--dc21   CIP

Copyright © 1998 National Court Reporters Association. All rights reserved.
No part of this book may be reproduced or transmitted in any form or by any
means, electronic or mechanical, including photocopying, recording, or by
any information storage or retrieval system without written permission from
the National Court Reporters Association.

ISBN: 1-881859-01-0

Preface

What This Book Is

One Word, Two Words, Hyphenated? seeks only to answer the title question — and to provide a quick answer on many words without need for further research. As a fringe benefit, you'll find help in spelling certain tricky words. For example, it includes many foreign words and phrases — chiefly French and Latin. In some instances this book will help with capitalization.

What This Book Isn't

First, it makes no claim to being comprehensive. It would need to be at least five times this long to begin to approach that goal. Second, though it has a smattering of definitions, it isn't a dictionary. And it doesn't claim to be consistent. Parts of speech are sometimes labeled (n., v., adj., etc.), but that's to differentiate noun from verb or adjective. Definitions mostly aim for clarification; sometimes I've included one simply because I found it interesting. To shorten things, I've often added after a noun "Hyphenate as adj." (Of course, *most* compound adjectives are hyphenated.) Also, to save space I sometimes put two words in the same family on one line (*bootleg/bootlegger*, for example).

Dictionaries disagree widely on hyphenation. In my research I settled on a consensus among the dictionaries I checked. (See Bibliography.) And the language keeps changing. There is a growing tendency to write as a solid word what used to be two or even three words. For instance, in older dictionaries you'll find *boyfriend* as one word but *girl friend* as two words. Now they're both written solid. Makes sense.

Another Point

Newspapers and magazines have their own style guides, and a writer for a publication needs to give such a style guide priority.

The basic purpose of hyphens and other punctuation marks is to make reading easier. If we're aware of the punctuation as we read, chances are there is something wrong with it. Thus we write "a three-year-old child," but hyphenating "a child three-years-old" is a waste of good hyphens, clutters up the sentence, and gives the reader a slight jolt.

John Benbow of Oxford University Press warned, "If you take hyphens seriously, you will surely go mad." That may well be true. But without being hyphen-happy, let's aim for consistency and a readable style, hyphenating or not in conformity with the best modern practice.

History and Credits

Earlier versions of this book were snapped up by the nation's court reporters, many of whom pronounced *One Word* their favorite reference work. It is our hope that journalists and other writers, editors, secretaries, et al., will also find it valuable. Why should court reporters have all the luck?

To help with the preparation of this book, two retired court reporters (Harold Berman of Bayside, N.Y., and William Boniface of Bethesda, Md.) and practicing reporter Eugenie H. Fitzhugh of Brockton, Mass., gave me invaluable assistance. They helped proofread, suggested further entries, and argued with me on some words. I'm extremely grateful for their help.

Mary Louise Gilman
Duxbury, Mass.

Important Note

Initially, I keyed into my computer *both* noun and verb forms in such words as *break-in* (n.), *break in* (v.); *breakout* (n.), *break out* (v.). But it soon became clear that this would make the book intolerably long. Besides, no halfway literate person would write "He tried to break-in" or "My skin began to breakout."

Thus in only a few cases will you find a short verb/adverb listed. For example, though the nouns *checkout* and *checkup* appear, just assume that you'll automatically write as two words the verb *check* and any adverb that follows.

—M.L.G.

Bibliography

The Random House Dictionary of the English Language, Unabridged, Second Edition, 1987.

The Random House Compact Unabridged Dictionary, Special Second Edition, 1996.

The American Heritage Dictionary of the English Language, Third Edition, 1992.

The American Heritage College Dictionary, Third Edition, 1993.

Webster's New Universal Unabridged Dictionary, Deluxe Second Edition, Simon and Schuster, 1979.

Merriam-Webster's Collegiate Dictionary, Tenth Edition, 1993.

Black's Law Dictionary, Fifth Edition, West Publishing Company, 1979.

Chambers Science and Technology Dictionary, 1988.

Encyclopedia of Nautical Knowledge, Cornell Maritime Press Inc., 1953.

McGraw-Hill Dictionary of Scientific and Technical Terms, Third Edition, McGraw-Hill, 1984.

Building Trades Dictionary, American Technical Publishers Inc., 1989.

A

abeam (Nautical)
able-bodied (adj.)
A-bomb
aborning (adv.): "The idea
    died aborning."
about-face (n.)
about face (interjec.):
    Military command to per-
    form an about-face.
aboveboard
aboveground
abovementioned, also
    above-mentioned
absentminded
absent without leave
abstract of title
abuilding
a cappella (It.): Without
    instrumental accompani-
    ment.
acaudal
access code
accident-prone
accounts payable
accounts receivable
AC/DC
ace high (adj.)
ace in the hole
acey-deucy: Form of
    backgammon.
acid dust
acid-fast
acid-forming
acidhead
acid rain
acid rock
acid-tongued
acid trip
ack-ack

acre-foot
acre-inch
across-the-board (adj.)
act call
act curtain
action grant
action line
action potential
activewear
act of God
acupressure
acupuncture
acute angle
acute-care (adj.)
ad damnum (L.)
added-value tax
addlebrained
addlepated
add-on (n.)
à deux (F.): With just two
    persons present. [Don't
    confuse with adieu!]
ad hoc (L.)
ad hominem (L.)
ad infinitum (L.)
ad lib (adv.)
ad-lib (adj., v.): "He gave an
    ad-lib speech."
    "He ad-libbed his speech."
    "He spoke ad lib."
ad litem (L.)
adman
ad nauseam (L.)
ad valorem (L.)
aerogram
afebrile
aforementioned
aforesaid
aforethought
a fortiori (L.)
A-frame
Afro-American

afterbeat
afterbirth
afterburner
aftercare
afterclap
afterdeck
after-dinner (adj.)
aftereffect
afterglow
aftergrowth
afterguard (Nautical)
afterheat
after-hours (adj.)
afterimage
afterlife
aftermath
aftermost (adj.): Farthest aft.
afterpains
afterpiece
after-shave (adj.)
aftershock
aftertaste
after-tax (adj.; e.g., an
    after-tax profit)
afterthought
afterward/afterwards
afterword
afterwork (adj.)
afterworld
afteryears
aftmost (Nautical)
agape
agate line
agateware
age group
agelong
Agent Orange
agent provocateur (F.)
age of consent
age-old
agitprop (Russ.): Propaganda.
aglare

agleam
agley (Scot.)
aglimmer
aglitter
à go-go
agribusiness
agrochemical
agro-economic
agro-industrial
agro-industry
ahold (n.): Hold (preferable).
aide-de-camp (F.)
aide-mémoire (F.)
AIDS-related complex
AIDS-related virus
air alert
air arm
air attaché
air bag
air ball (Basketball)
air base
air battery
air bed
air bell
airbill: Air waybill.
air bladder
air blast
airboat
airborne
air brake
air brick
airbrush
airbus
air casing
air cell
air chamber
air coach
air cock
air-condition (v.)
air-conditioned (adj.)
air conditioning [Hyphen-
    ate as adj.]

air conduction
air-cool (v.)
air-cooled (adj.)
air cover
aircraft
aircrew
aircrewman
air curtain
air cushion
air-cushion vehicle
air dam
airdate: Scheduled date of a broadcast.
air door
air drill
airdrop
air-dry (v., adj.)
air duct
airfare
airfield
air fleet
airflow
airfoil
air force
airframe
airfreight (n., v.)
air freshener
airglow
air gun
air hammer
airhead
air hole
airhose
air hunger
air jacket
air lane
air-launched cruise missile
air layering
air letter
airlift
airlifter
airlight (n.)

airline (n.): Transportation system.
air-line (adj.)
air line: A straight line through the air between two points.
airliner
air lock (n.)
air-lock (v.)
air log (n.)
air-logged (adj.)
airmail
airman
air marshal
air mass
air mattress
air meter
air mile
air-minded
airmobile
airpack (n.)
airpark (n.)
airpipe
air piracy
airplane
airplay
air plot
air pocket
air police
airpower
air pressure
air pump
air raid [Hyphenate as adj.]
air rifle
air rights
air route
air sac
air scoop
airshed
airship (n.)
air-ship (v.)
airshow

air shower
airsick
airsickness
air sign
air-slake (v.)
air space
airspeed
air splint
airstream
air strike
airstrip
air switch
air taxi
airtight
airtime (Broadcasting)
air-to-air (adj.)
air-traffic control
air twist
airwash (v.)
airwaves
airway
air waybill
airworthy
airy-fairy (adj.)
aitchbone
akimbo
à la (F.): In the manner of.
à la carte
à la king
Al-Anon
Alateen
albeit
al dente (It.): Cooked until barely tender.
aleph-null: A cardinal number.
alewife
alfresco (It.; adj., adv.): In the open air.
Ali Baba
Alice-in-Wonderland (adj.): Unreal.

A-line
all along
all-American
all-around
all clear
all-day (adj.)
all-embracing
all-expense
alley cat
alley light
alley-oop (interjec.)
alleyway
all-fired (adj.)
all fours
all get-out
all hail (interjec.)
Allhallows Eve: Halloween.
all-important
all in all
all-inclusive
all-night (adj.)
all-nighter (n.)
all-or-none (adj.)
all-or-nothing (adj.)
all-out (adj.): "He made an all-out effort to win."
all out (adv.): "He went all out to win."
allover (adj.): "An allover pattern."
all over (adv.): "I ached all over."
all-points bulletin
all-powerful
all-purpose
all right (always two words)
all-round: All-around.
allspice
all-star
all-state
all-terrain vehicle
all-time

all together: Together; in concert. [See *altogether*.]
all told
all-weather
all-year
alma mater
almighty (cap when referring to God)
almond-eyed
almshouse
alongships
alongshore
alongside
a lot (always two words)
alpha and omega
alpha blocker
alpha decay
alpha globulin
alpha helix
alphanumeric
alpha particle
alpha ray
alpha receptor
alpha rhythm
alpha test
alpha waves
also-ran (n.)
altar boy
altarpiece
altar rail
alter ego (L.)
altocumulus: Cloud formation.
altogether (n.): Nude.
altogether (adv.): Wholly, completely; all told. [Don't confuse with *all together*.]
ambient air
amen corner
a mensa et thoro (L.): Literally from bed and board. (Divorce Law)

Amerindian (n., adj.)
amicus curiae (L.; pl. **amici curiae**)
amidships
amino acid
amino-acid dating
aminobenzene
amino group
amino resin
aminosugar
amoral
ampere-hour
Amtrak
amyl acetate
amyl group
anal-retentive (Psychology)
anchorman/anchorperson/anchorwoman
andante (It.): Musical direction.
AND gate (Computer Science)
andiron
AND NOT gate (Computer Science)
and/or
AND-OR circuit (Computer Science)
angel dust
angel food cake
angel hair
angina pectoris
angle iron
anglerfish
angle shot
Anglo-American
Anglo-French
Anglophile
Anglophobe
Anglo-Saxon
anklebone
ankle-deep (adj., adv.)

ankle jerk
Annie Oakley
anno Domini
answerback (n., adj.)
answering machine
antacid [No such word as
 antiacid!]
antebellum
antechamber
antedate
antediluvian
antemeridian: Occurring
 before noon.
ante meridiem: A.M.
antemortem
antenatal
antenuptial
antepenult
anteroom

ANTI- WORDS
NOTE: We list here only the
most common *anti-* words. If
the one you seek isn't given,
consult your dictionary. As a
rule of thumb, unless *anti-*
precedes the letter *i* or a
proper noun, write as one
word.
 antiabortion
 antiacid [No such word!
  It's *antacid.*]
 antiaircraft
 antiallergenic
 anti-American
 antibacterial
 antiballistic missile
 antibiotic
 antiblack
 antibody
 anti-British
 antibureaucratic

antibusiness
antibusing
anticarcinogenic
anti-Catholic
Antichrist: One who
 denies or opposes
 Christ.
anti-Christian
antichurch
anticigarette
anticlimactic
anticlimax
anticoagulant
anticolonialism
anticommunism/
 anticommunist
anticonglomerate
anticonservation
anticonsumerism
anticorporate
anticorrosive
anticorruption
anticrime
antidepressant
antidiscrimination
anti-English
antierotic
antiestablishment
antifascist
antifashionable
antifeminist
antifreeze
anti-French
antigen
anti-German
anti-G suit (Aeronautics)
antigun (adj.)
antigunners (n.)
antihero
antihistamine
anti-ideological
anti-inflammatory

anti-inflation
anti-intellectual
anti-Italian
anti-Jewish
antiknock
antilabor
antimanagement
antimarijuana
antimonopoly
anti-Nazi
anti-Negro
antinoise
antinuclear
antiobscenity
antiparty
antipasto: An appetizer.
antiperspirant
antipollution
antipoverty
antirape
anti-Russian
anti-Semitism
antisex
antismog
antismoking
antisocial
anti-Soviet
antispasmodic
antistatic
antitakeover
antitobacco
antitoxin
antitrust
antiunion
antiviral
antivivisection
antiwar
antiwhite
antiwoman

anymore (adv.): Any longer. (Regularly used in the neg-

ative: "I don't do it anymore"; also now used in positive construction: "I shop at Johnson's anymore.")

any more: Rule of thumb: Use as two words before a noun or the word *than*. ("We don't have any more men." "I don't like it any more than you do.")

anyone (pron.)

any one: Always two words preceding a noun or following a preposition. ("Any one person"; "at any one time"; "in any one period.")

anyplace (adv.): Anywhere. (But "We can build in any place we choose.")

anytime (adv.): At any time whatever. ("We can go anytime.")

any time: Always two words when preceded by *at*. ("I can go at any time.")

anyway (adv.): In any case; anyhow.

any way: Two words when preceded by *in*. ("In any way possible.")

anywise (adv.): In any way whatever.

A-OK (adv., adj.): Definitely OK.

A one or **A-1** (adj.): First-rate.

ape-man

Apgar score

apiece: For each one; individually.

applecart
applejack
appleknocker
apple-pie (adj.)
apple-polish (v.)
applesauce
après-ski (n., adj.)
April Fools' Day
a priori (L.)
apron string(s)
apropos
aquacade
aquaculture
Aqua-Lung™
aqua pura (L.)
aqua vitae (L.)
aqueous humor
aquifer
aquiver
Arabic numerals
arborvitae
archangel
arch beam
archbishop
archenemy
archetype
archfiend
archrival
archway
arc lamp
area code
area rug
areaway
aright (adv.): Rightly; correctly.
armband
armchair
armful
armhole
armload
armlock
armpatch

armpit
armrest
arm's-length (adj.)
arm-twisting
arm-wrestle (v.)
arm wrestling
around-the-clock (adj.)
arrivederci (It.): Good-bye.
arrowhead
arrowroot
art deco
art film
art form
art nouveau
artsy-craftsy
artwork
asexual
ash-blond (adj.)
ashcan: A style of painting (sometimes capitalized).
ash can: Receptacle for refuse.
ashtray
assbackwards
assembly line
assemblyman/ assemblywoman
asshole
assigned risk
ass-kick (v.)
ass kissing
astraddle
Astroturf™
at bat
at-home (n.): A reception given at one's home.
athwartships
attaboy
attaché case
attagirl
attention-getting
attention span

attorney-at-law
attorney general
atypical
au contraire (F.)
au courant (F.): Fully famil-
   iar; conversant.
audiocassette
audio-lingual (adj.)
audiotape
audiovisual(s)
au gratin (F.)
au jus (F.)
auld lang syne
au naturel (F.; adj.)
au pair (F.)
au revoir (F.)
autobahn: A German
   expressway.
autobus
autoeroticism
autofocus
autoimmune
autointoxication
autoloader (Firearms)
automaker
automated teller machine
   (ATM)
autosuggestion
autoworker
avant-garde (F.; n., adj.)
aweigh
a while (n.)
awhile (adv.): Note that *for* is
   built into the adverb
   awhile. "Stay awhile."
   "Stay for a while and rest
   awhile." "I'll return in a
   while." "I'll see you after a
   while." "It was quite a
   while ago." "A while ago he
   said it would take a while."
   "They talked awhile."

aw-shucks
axletree
a-yuh (interjec., New
   England)
azo dye
azo group

B

baba au rhum
babe in the woods
baby boom/baby boomer
baby doll
baby-faced
baby grand
babyproof
baby's breath
baby-sit/baby-sat
baby-sitter/baby-sitting
baby talk
bachelor's degree
backache
back-alley (adj.)
back and fill (v.)
back and forth [Hyphenate
   as adj.]
backbite
backboard
backbone
backbreaking
back burner
back country (n.)
backcourt (Basketball)
backcross (v., Genetics)
backdate (v.)
back door (n.)
backdoor (adj.)
backdown (n.)
back down (v.)
backdrop
backer-up (pl. backers-up)

backfield
backfill
backfire
back formation or
   back-formation
backgammon
background
backgrounder: Briefing for
   the press.
backhand/backhanded
backhaul
backhoe
backhouse
backlash
backlight/backlighting
backlist (n., v.)
backlisted
backload
backlog
back lot (Movies)
back mutation (Genetics)
back order (n.)
backorder (v.)
backpack/backpacker
back-patting
backpedal (v.)
backplate
backrest
back road
back room (n.)
backroom (adj.)
backrub
back scratcher
back seat or backseat (n.)
backseat (adj.)
backseat driver
backside-front (adv.)
backside-to (adv.)
backslap/backslapper
backslide
backspace
backstage (adv., adj.)

back stairs (n.)
backstairs (adj.)
backstay
backstitch
backstop
back street (n.)
backstreet (adj.)
backstretch
backstroke
backswing
back talk
back to back [Hyphenate as
   adj.]
back-to-basics (adj.)
backtrack
backup (n., adj.)
backwash
backwater
backwind (v.)
backwoods/backwoodsy
back yard or backyard
bad actor
badass (n., adj.)
bad blood
bad hair day
badlands
bad-mouth (v.)
bad-tempered (adj.)
bag lady
bagman: Dishonest official.
bail bond
bailout
bait and switch [Hyphenate
   as adj.]
bakegoods
bake-off (n.)
baker's dozen
bakeshop
bakeware
balance sheet
bald-faced (adj.): Bold-faced;
   barefaced.

baldhead (n.): Baldheaded person.
baldheaded
ball and chain
ball-and-socket joint
ball bearing
ball-buster
ballcarrier (Football)
ball club
ball cock
ball game
ball of fire
ball of wax
ballot box
ballpark (n., adj.)
ball-peen hammer
ballpoint
ballroom
ballyhoo
bamboo curtain (often capitalized)
banana oil
banana republic
Band-Aid™
bandbox
bandleader
bandmaster
band mill
band saw
band shell
bandsman
bandstand
bandwagon
bandwidth
bandy-legged
bangtail: A racehorse.
bang-up (adj.): First-rate.
bank account
bankbook
bank card
bank draft
bank note

bankroll (n., v.)
bantamweight
bar-and-grill (n.)
barbecue
barbed wire, also **barb wire**
barbell
barbershop
bar car
bar code
bareback
bareboned
bare bones [Hyphenate as adj.]
barefaced
barefoot
barehanded
bareheaded
bare-knuckled (adj., adv.)
barelegged
barf bag
barfly
bar girl
barhop
barkeep/barkeeper
barmaid/barman
bar mitzvah (Heb.)
barnburner
barn dance
barn owl
barn raising
barnstorm
barnyard
barrelful
barrelhead
barrelhouse
barrel organ
barrel roll (n.)
barrel-roll (v.)
barroom
barstool
bartender
basal cell

11

baseboard
baseborn (adj.): Of humble
  parentage.
baseburner
base coat
base level
baseline
base pair (Genetics)
base pairing
base pay
base rate
base runner
basis point
basket case
basketwork
bas mitzvah (Heb.):
  Feminine equivalent of
  bar mitzvah.
bas-relief
bassackwards
bass clef
bass drum
basset hound
bass viol
batboy/batgirl
bathhouse
bathmat
bathrobe
bath salts
bath towel
bathtub
bathwater
batman
battered child syndrome
battering ram
battle-ax
battle cry
battlefield
battlefront
battle line
battle royal
battle-scarred

battle wagon
bawdyhouse
bawl out
bay rum
bay window
B battery
B cell
beachball
beachboy
beach buggy
beachcomber
beachfront
beachhead
beadwork
beady-eyed
be-all and end-all: Prime
  cause.
beam-ends (Nautical)
beanbag
bean counter
bean curd
beanpole
bean pot
bean sprouts
bearcat
bear claw
bear hug (n.)
bearskin
beatnik
beat-up (adj.)
beaucoup (F.; adj.)
beau geste (F.): A graceful
  gesture.
beau monde (F.): World of
  high society.
beauty parlor
beauty spot
Beaux-Arts (F.): Fine arts.
beaverboard
bed and board
bed-and-breakfast
bed board

bedbug
bedchamber
bed check
bedclothes
beddy-bye
bedfast
bedfellow
bedmate
bed of roses
bedpan
bedpost
bed rest
bedridden
bedrock
bedroll
bedsheet
bedside manner
bed-sitter (Brit.)
bedsore
bedspread
bedstead
bed table
bedtime
bedwetter/bedwetting
beefcake
beefeater
beefed-up (adj.)
beef up (v.)
beehive
beekeeper
beeline
beeswax
behindhand
behind-the-scenes (adj.)
bel canto (It.): Style of operatic singing.
belladonna: Poisonous plant.
bell-bottom(s)
bellboy
bell captain
belles-lettres (F.): Literary studies and writings.

bellhop
bell jar
bell-shaped curve
belltower
bellwether [Not *bellweather*!]
bellyache
bellyband
bellyboard (surf riding)
bellybutton
belly dance/belly dancer
belly flop (n.)
belly-flop (v.)
bellyful
belly laugh
belly-up (adj.): Done for; bankrupt.
belly-up (v.): To move next to.
belly-wash
belowdecks
belowground
below stairs (n.)
belt line: A transportation system.
belt-tightening
beltway
benchmark: Standard of excellence.
bench mark (Surveying)
benchwarmer
bench warrant
beriberi
best-case (adj.)
best-efforts selling
best in show: Award to a dog, etc.
best man
bestseller (n.)
bestsellerdom
bestselling (adj.)
beta-blocker
beta cell
beta particle

13

beta-receptor
beta rhythm
beta wave
betel nut
bête noire (F.): Detested person or thing.
better half
better-off (adj.)
betweenbrain: Diencephalon.
between-deck
betweentimes
biannual: Occurring twice a year.
biathlon
bib and tucker
Bible belt
biennial: Occurring every two years; continuing or lasting for two years.
Big Apple
big band
big bang theory
big beat
Big Board: New York Stock Exchange.
big-boned
big game
big gun
bighead/bigheaded
big-hearted
bighorn: Wild sheep.
big house: Penitentiary.
big league [Hyphenate as adj.]
bigmouth/bigmouthed
big name [Hyphenate as adj.]
big shot [Hyphenate as adj.]
big-ticket (adj.): High-priced.
big time [Hyphenate as adj.]
big top

big wheel
bigwig
bile duct
bile salt
bi-level
bilge water
billboard
billet-doux (F.; pl. billets-doux): Love letter.
bill of fare
bill of goods
bill of health
bill of lading
bill of sale
billy club
billy goat
bimonthly
binary code
bindle stiff
bind over
binge-purge syndrome: Bulimia.
bioassay
biodegradable
biofeedback
birdbath
birdbrain/birdbrained
bird cage
birdcall
bird dog (n.)
bird-dog (v.): To watch closely; to seek out.
bird-dogging (n.)
birdhouse
bird of prey
birdseed
bird's-eye view
birdshot
birdsong
bird-watch (v.)
bird watcher
bird watching

birth certificate
birth control [Hyphenate as adj.]
birth date
birthday suit
birthmark
birth mother
birthplace
birthrate
birthright
bisexual
bite-size
bitter end
bittersweet
biweekly
biyearly
blabbermouth
black-and-blue (adj.)
black and tan (n.): A black-and-tan animal.
black-and-tan (adj.)
black and white (n.): A drawing or print done in black and white.
black-and-white (adj.)
black art: Magic.
black-bag (adj.)
blackball (v.)
black belt
black book
black box
Black English
black eye (n.)
blackface (Theater)
blackguard: A scoundrel.
blackhearted
black hole
blackjack
blacklist (n., v.)
black magic
blackmail
black market (n.)

black-market (v.)
black-marketeer
blackout (n.)
black out (v.)
black sheep
blacksmith
black tie [Hyphenate as adj.]
blacktop (n., adj., v.)
black widow spider
blah-blah-blah
blameworthy
blank check
blankety-blank (adj., adv.)
blank verse
Blarney stone
blast cell
blastoff (n.)
blast off (v.)
bleary-eyed
bleeding heart
bleu cheese, also blue cheese: The best comes from France.
blind alley
blind date
blindfold
blindman's buff (sometimes bluff)
blind pig
blind side (n.)
blindside (v.): Sports term.
blind spot
blind tiger
blind trust
blitzkrieg
block and tackle
blockbuster/blockbusting
block grant
blockhead
bloc-vote (v.)
blood-alcohol
blood-and-guts (adj.)

15

blood and thunder (n.)
blood bank
bloodbath
blood brother
blood cell
blood count
bloodcurdler/bloodcurdling
blood heat
bloodletting
blood level
bloodline
blood meal
bloodmobile
blood money
blood plasma
blood poisoning
blood pressure
blood-red (adj.)
blood serum
bloodshed
bloodshot
bloodstain/bloodstained
bloodstock
bloodstream
bloodsucker
blood sugar
blood test
bloodthirsty
blood type/blood typing
blood vessel
blood work
blot out
blow-by-blow
blow-dry
blowgun
blowhard (n.): Braggart.
blowhole
blown-up (adj.)
blowoff (n.)
blowout (n.)
blowpipe
blowtorch

blowup (n.)
blue baby
bluebeard
blue-black
blue blood (n.)
blue-blooded (adj.)
blue book
blue cheese [See also bleu cheese.]
blue chip [Hyphenate as adj.]
blue-collar (adj.)
blue flu: Sick-out (police officers).
bluegrass
bluejacket: A sailor.
blue jeans [Note: This is often written as one word.]
blue law(s)
blueline (Printing)
blue line (Ice Hockey)
blue moon
bluenose (n.)
blue-pencil (v.)
blue-plate (adj.)
blueprint
blue-ribbon (adj.)
blue-sky (adj.)
bluestocking
blue streak
B-movie
B'nai B'rith
board-certified (adj.)
board foot
boardinghouse
boarding school
board of trade
boardroom
boardwalk
boatbuilder
boat deck

boat hook
boathouse
boatman
boat people
boatswain (tricky pronuncia-
tion!)
boat train
boatwright
boatyard
bobby socks (also bobby
sox)
bobbysoxer
bock beer
body art
body bag
bodybuilder/bodybuilding
body count
body English
bodyguard
body language
body politic
body-search (v.)
body shop
body snatcher
bodysuit
bodywear
bodywork
bogeyman or bogyman [See
also boogeyman.]
boiled oil
boilermaker
boilerplate
boiler room
boiling point
boldface (n.): Type.
bold-faced (adj.): Impudent;
set in boldface.
boll weevil
bollworm
bolo tie (also bola tie)
bolt-action (adj.)
bomb bay

bombed-out
bombproof
bombshell
bombsight
bona fide (adj.)
bona fides (n.)
bondholder
bondsman
bone china
bone-crushing
bone-dry
bonehead
bone-marrow transplant
bone meal
boneyard
bon mot (F.): Witticism.
bon vivant (F.): A person of
cultivated tastes; epicure.
bon voyage (F.)
boo-boo
boob tube
booby hatch
booby trap
boogeyman or boogerman:
Bogeyman.
boogie-woogie
boo-hoo
bookbinder/bookbinding
book burning
bookcase
book club
bookmaker/bookmaking
bookmark
bookmobile
book review
bookseller/bookselling
book share
bookshelf
bookshop
bookstore
book value
bookworm

boom box
boom shot
boomtown
boondocks
boondoggle
booster shot
boot camp
bootleg/bootlegger
bootlick/bootlicker
bootstrap
boozed-up (adj.)
borderline
borehole
boresight (v., Firearms)
boresighting (n., Firearms)
bore-siting: The siting of boreholes (construction or drilling).
boric acid
born-again (adj.)
borrow pit
borscht circuit
bosom friend
bossman/bosslady
bottle baby
bottle-feed/bottle-fed
bottleneck
bottle-nosed dolphin
bottlewasher
bottom line
bottom out (v.)
bottoms up
bottom-up (adj.)
bottom-up programming
bounceback (n.)
bounty hunter
bow front
bowknot
bowlegged
bowline (Nautical)
bowling alley
bowling green

bowl over
bowsprit
bowstring
bow tie
bowwow
boxboard
boxcar
box lunch
box office [Hyphenate as adj.]
box score
box seat
boychik or boychick (Yid.): Boy.
boyfriend
boy scout
boy toy
boy wonder
brachial plexus
brainchild
brain-dead (adj.)
brain death
brain drain
brainpower
brainstorm/brainstorming
brainteaser
brain trust
brainwash/brainwashing
brain wave
brake fluid
brake lining
brakeman
brake pedal
brake shoe
branch water [goes well with bourbon]
brand name
brand-new
Brand X
brass band
brass hat
brass knuckles

brass ring
brass-rubbing
brass tacks
brazen-faced
Brazil nut
bread and butter
  [Hyphenate as adj.]
breadbasket
breadboard
breadbox
breadcrumb
bread knife
bread line
breadstick
breadwinner
breakaway (n., adj.)
break dance (n.)
break dancing
breakdown (n.)
break-even (adj.)
breakfront
break-in (n.)
breakneck (adj.)
breakout (n.)
breakpoint or break point
breakthrough (n.)
breakup (n.)
breakwater
breast-beating
breast-feed/breast-fed
breastplate
breaststroke
breathtaking
bred-in-the-bone: Deep-
  rooted.
breech baby
breech birth
breechloader (Firearms)
breeding ground
breezeway
bric-a-brac (F.)
brickbat

bricklayer
brickyard
bridgehead
bridge loan
bridgework
bridle path
briefcase
bringdown (n.)
brinkmanship
Bristol board
broadband
broad-based
broad beam
broad-brush (adj.): General;
  nonspecific.
broad jump
broadloom
broad-minded
broadside
broad-spectrum (adj.)
broken-down (adj.)
broken-field (adj., Football)
broken heart
brokenhearted
broken-winded
Bronx cheer
broomstick
brouhaha
browbeat (v.)
browbeaten (adj.)
brown-bag (v., adj.)
brown bagger (n.)
brown-bagging
brown belt
Brownie point
brown-nose (v.)
brownout
brownstone
brush fire [Hyphenate as
  adj.]
brush-off (n.)
brushup (n.)

brushwork
bubble bath
bubblegum
bubblehead
bubbletop (adj.)
bucket brigade
bucket seat
bucket shop
buckeye
buck fever
buck passer
buckshot
buckskin
buck slip
bucktooth (n.; pl. buckteeth)
bucktoothed
buck up
buckwheat
buddy-buddy
buddy seat
buddy system
buffer state
buffer zone
bugaboo
bug-eyed
bughouse
bug-juice
bug off (v.)
bugout (n.)
bug out (v.)
building block
buildup (n.)
built-in (adj.)
built-up (adj.)
bulkhead
bulldozer
bullethead
bulletproof
bull fiddle
bullfight/bullfighter
bullheaded/bullheadedness
bullmastiff

bull-necked
bull pen
bull ring
bull session
bull's-eye
bullshit
bull terrier
bullwhip
bullyboy
bully pulpit
bullyrag: To intimidate by
    bullying.
bumper sticker
bumper-to-bumper (adj.)
bumpoff (n.)
bump off (v.)
bum rap
bum's rush
bungee jumping
bunghole
bunk bed
bunkhouse
bunkmate
burden of proof
burglar alarm
burglarproof
burned-out or burnt-out
    (adj.)
burnout (n.)
busboy
bushbeater
bush league [Hyphenate as
    adj.]
bushwhack (v.)
bushwhacker (n.)
bushy-tailed
businesslike
businessman/
    businesswoman
busman's holiday
bust-up (n.)
busybody

busywork
butter-and-egg man
butterball
butterfat
butterfingered/
    butterfingers
buttinsky
butt joint
button-down, also
    buttoned-down (adj.)
buttoned-up (adj.)
buyback (n.)
buy-down (n.)
buy-in (n.)
buyoff (n.)
buyout (n.)
buyup (n.)
buzz saw
buzzword
by-and-by (n.): Some future
    time or occasion.
by and by (adv.): After a
    while; soon.
by and large
bye-bye
by-election
bylaw
byline
bypass
by-play
by-product
byroad
bystander
by-talk
byway
byword
by-your-leave (n.)

C

cabdriver
cabin class
cabinetmaker/
    cabinetmaking
cabin fever
cable car
cab-over (n.): Vehicle with
    the cab located over the
    engine. (Also adj.)
cabstand
cakes and ale
cakewalk
callback (n.)
call box
caller ID
call girl
call-in (radio and TV)
call letters
call loan
call market
call-out (n.)
call-up (n.)
call waiting
camcorder
camelback
cameraman
camera-shy
camp follower
campground
campout (n.)
campsite
campstool
camp stove
camshaft
cam wheel
Canada goose
cancan
candleholder
candlelight/candlelit

candlepin
candlepower
candlestick
candlewood
Candygram™
candy striper
canker sore
cannonball
can of worms
canon law
capital gains
capital stock
Capitol Hill: The U.S.
    Congress.
cap screw
capstone
carbarn
car bomb
carbon black
carbon copy
carbon-date (v.)
carbon dating (n.)
carbon paper
cardboard
card-carrying
cardholder
card-key
cardplayer
card shark
cardsharp
career woman
carefree
caregiver
CARE package or care
    package
caretaker
careworn
carjacker/carjacking
carload
carmaker
carnal knowledge
carpal tunnel syndrome

car park
carpetbag/carpetbagger
carpet sweeper
car pool (n.)
carpool (v.)
carpooler/carpooling
carport
carrot-and-stick (adj.)
carrot-top
carryall
carryback
carryforward
carry-in (adj.)
carrying charge
carrying(s)-on: Excited or
    immoral behavior.
carry-on (n., adj.)
carryout (n., adj.)
carryover (n.)
carsick/carsickness
carte blanche (F.)
cartop (adj.)
cartridge belt
cartwheel (n., v.)
car wash
casebook
case goods
caseharden
case history
case law
caseload
case study
casework/caseworker
cash-and-carry (adj.)
cash bar
cashbook
cashbox
cash cow
cash crop
cash flow
cash-in (n.): Redemption, as
    of mutual-fund shares.

cash-out (n.): Direct cash payment or cash profit.
cash value
castaway (n., adj.)
caste mark (in India)
cast iron [Hyphenate as adj.]
castoff (n., adj.)
casus belli (L.)
cat-and-dog (adj.)
cat and mouse [Hyphenate as adj.]
catawampus
catbird seat
catboat
cat burglar
catcall
catchall (n.)
catch-as-catch-can (adj., adv.)
catch basin
catch phrase: Slogan.
Catch-22, also **catch-22**
catch-up (n., adj.)
catchword
cater-corner, also **catty-corner, kitty corner**
cater-cornered, also **kitty-cornered**
caterwaul (n., v.)
catfight
catgut
cathode-ray tube
cathouse
catlike
catnap
catnapper (n.): One who takes catnaps; one who steals cats.
cat-o'-nine-tails
CAT scan
cat's cradle
cat's-eye: A gem.

catskinner: Operator of a machine with caterpillar treads.
cat's-paw: A dupe.
cattle call: A mass audition, as of actors.
cattle car
cattleman
catty-cornered: See *cater-cornered.*
cause-and-effect (adj.)
cause célèbre (F.)
causeway
caveat emptor (L.)
cave dweller
cave-in (n.)
caveman
CD-ROM
CD single
cease-and-desist order
cease-fire (n.)
cellblock
cellmate
cell plate
cell wall
cement mixer
census taker
centerboard (Nautical)
center field
centerfold
centerline, also **center line**
centerpiece
center spread (Journalism)
central heating
Central Standard Time
cerebrospinal
cesspool
c'est la vie (F.): That's life.
cha-cha
chafing dish
chain drive
chain gang

chain letter
chain-link fence
chain mail
chain of command
chain saw (n.)
chain-saw (v.)
chain-smoke (v.)
chain-smoker (n.)
chain stitch (n.)
chainstitch (v.)
chain store
chairlift
chaise longue (F.; *not* chaise lounge.)
chalkboard: Blackboard.
chalk line
chambermaid
chamber music
changemaker
change of heart
change of life
change of pace
change of venue
changeover (n.)
change-up (Baseball)
channel-surf (v.)
channel surfer (n.)
channel-surfing (n.)
chapter and verse
character witness
charbroil
charge account
chargeback (Banking)
charge card
charge-coupled device
chargé d'affaires (F.): Subordinate diplomat.
charge-off (n.)
charge plate
charley horse
charmed life
charter member

chateaubriand (F.)
chatterbox
cheapjack (n., adj.)
cheap shot
cheapskate
checkback: Verification.
checkbook
checkerboard
check-in (n.)
checklist
check mark (n.)
checkmark (v.)
checkmate
checkoff (n.)
checkout (n.)
check-over (n.)
checkpoint
checkroom
checkup (n.)
check valve
checkwriter: A machine, not a person.
cheddar cheese
cheekbone
cheerer-upper
cheerleader
cheeseboard
cheeseburger
cheesecake
cheesecloth
cheeseparing: Something insignificant.
chef-d'oeuvre (F.; pl. chefs-d'oeuvre)
chemin de fer (F.): A version of baccarat.
chemoreception/ chemoreceptor
chemosensory
chemosurgery
chemotherapy
cherry bomb

cherry picker
cherrystone: Clam.
Cheshire cat
chessboard
chessman
chest of drawers
chewing gum
chew out
chichi
chicken-and-egg (adj.)
chicken coop
chicken feed
chicken-hearted
chicken-livered
chickenpox
chicken wire
chickpea
chief of staff
chief of state
child abuse
childbearing
childbed
childbirth
childcare, also child-care
child labor
childlike
childproof
child's play
child support
chiliburger
chili con carne
chili dog
chili sauce
chiller-diller
chill factor
chimneypiece
chimney pot
chimney sweep
china closet
chinaware
chinbone
chinwag (n., v.)

chipboard
chipped beef
chip shot (Golf)
chitchat
chloral hydrate
chockablock
chock-full
choirboy/choirgirl
choirloft
choirmaster
choke hold, also chokehold
chop-chop: Quickly.
chophouse
chopping block
chop shop: Garage where
   stolen cars are dismantled.
chopstick
chop suey
chorus boy/chorus girl
chowchow: A relish.
chow chow: Breed of dog.
chowderhead
chowhound
chow mein
Christmastide
Christmastime
chuck-a-luck: A dice game.
chuckhole
chuck wagon
chug-a-lug/chug-a-lugged
chump change
churchgoer
church school
churchwarden
chute-the-chute (n.)
chutzpah (Yid.; also
   chutzpa): Nerve, gall.
cigar-store Indian
cinder block
cinéma vérité (F.)
circuit board
circuit breaker

circuit court
circuit rider
circular saw
cirrocumulus: A cloud.
citizen's arrest
citizens band: Two-way
  radio service.
city council
city desk
city editor
city room
cityscape
city slicker
city-state (n.)
citywide
civic center
civic-minded
civil defense
civil rights
civil service
claim-jumper
clambake
clampdown (n.)
clamshell
clansman/clanswoman
clapboard
claptrap
class act
class action
class-conscious (adj.)
class consciousness (n.)
classroom
classwork
claw hammer (n.)
clawhammer (adj.)
clay pigeon
clean-cut (adj.)
clean-handed (adj.)
clean hands (n.)
cleaning woman
clean-limbed (adj.)
clean-living (adj.)

cleanout (n.)
clean room: An area free of
  contaminants (for lab
  work, etc.).
clean-shaven (adj.)
clean sweep
cleanup (n.)
clear-air turbulence
clear-coating: Automobile
  painting technique.
clear-cut (adj., v.)
clear-eyed
clearheaded
clearinghouse
cleft palate
cliff dweller
cliff-hanger (n.)
cliff-hanging (adj.)
climate control
climb-down (n.): A retreat.
clinker-built (adj.)
clinkety-clank
clipboard
clip-clop
clip joint
clip-on (adj.)
clip-out (adj.)
clippety-clop
clipsheet (Journalism)
cloak-and-dagger (adj.)
cloakroom
clocklike
clockmaker
clock radio
clock-watcher
clockwise
clockwork
clodhopper
clop-clop
close-at-hand (adj.)
close-by (adj.)
close call (n.)

close-cropped (adj.)
closed book
closed-captioned
closed-circuit television
closed corporation
closed-door (adj.)
closed-end investment
company
closed-loop (adj.)
closed-minded or
close-minded (adj.)
closedown (n.)
closed season
closed shop
closed stack (Library
Science)
closefisted (adj.)
close-fitting
close-grained (Wood)
close-hauled (Nautical; adj.,
adv.)
close-in (adj.)
close-knit
close-lipped
close-mouthed
close order
close-order drill
closeout (n.): A sale.
close quarters
close quote
close shave
close shot (Movies, TV)
close-up (n., adj.)
clothbound (Books)
clothesbasket
clotheshorse
clothesline
clothes moth
clothespin
clothes tree
cloudburst
cloud-capped

cloud chamber (Physics)
cloud cover
cloudland
cloud nine
cloud seeding
cloven hoof, also cloven
foot
cloven-hoofed
cloverleaf
club car
club chair
clubfoot/clubfooted
clubhouse
clubroom
club soda
cluster bomb
clutch bag

CO- WORDS
NOTE: Although this list
doesn't contain all possible
co- words, we trust it covers
those you're likely to
encounter.
coact/coactive
coaction
coagent
coanchor (n., v.)
coauthor
coaxial
cobelligerent
cochair
cochairman
coconspirator
cocounsel
codefendant
codirect/codirector
codiscover
co-edition (but
coedit/coeditor)
coeducational
coequal

coeval
coexecutor/coexecutrix
coexist
cofounder
cofunction
cogeneration
cohabit
coheir
cohost/cohostess
coinsurance/coinsurer
coinventor
comaker
comanage
comingle: Commingle.
co-occur/co-occurred
co-occurrence
co-official
co-op (n., adv., v.)
co-oped/co-oping
cooperate/cooperation
co-opt
co-own/co-owner
copartner/copartnership
copayment
copilot
copresident
coproduce/coproducer
copublish/copublisher
corecipient
coreference/coreferential
corespondent: Especially
   in a divorce case.
cosign/cosigner
cosignatory
cosponsor/
   cosponsorship
costar/costarring
cotrustee
covariance/covariant
coworker
cowrite
§

coalbin
coal car
coal field
coal gas
coalhole
coal mine
coal tar
coarse-grained
coastal plain
coast-guard cutter
coastland
coastline
coast-to-coast (adj.)
coastwise
coatdress
coat hanger
coat of arms
coatrack
coatroom
coattail
coaxial cable
cobalt blue
cobblestone
cobweb
cochlear implant
cock-a-doodle-doo
cockamamie
cock-and-bull story
cockcrow
cocked hat
cockeyed
cockfight
cock of the walk
cockpit
cockscomb
cocksure
cocoa butter
codebook
code dating
code name (n.)
code-name (v.)
code-switching

code word
code work
cod-liver oil
coed
coffee break
coffeecake
coffee-colored
coffeehouse (n.): A public place serving coffee.
coffeehouse (v.): To make misleading gestures, etc., in playing cards.
coffee klatsch (n.): Social gathering.
coffee-klatsch (v.): To get together for a coffee klatsch.
coffee maker
coffee mill
coffeepot
coffee shop
coffee-table book
cofferdam
cognoscenti (pl.); cognoscente (sing.)
coil spring
coin-operated
cokehead
coke oven
cold-blooded
cold cash
cold chisel (n.)
cold-chisel (v.)
cold comfort
cold cuts
cold duck
cold-eyed
cold feet
cold fish
cold-hearted
cold pack (n.)
cold-pack (v.)

cold-roll (v.)
cold shoulder (n.)
cold-shoulder (v.)
cold snap
cold sore
cold storage
cold turkey (n.)
cold type
cold war
cold-water (adj.)
cold wave
coleslaw
collarbone
collect call
collision course
color bar
colorbearer
color-blind
color blindness
color code
color-coordinated
colorfast
color guard
color line
colorslide
combat-ready
combat zone
comb-out (n.)
comb-over: Man's hair style.
comeback (n.)
comedown (n.)
come-hither (adj.)
come-on (n.)
comeuppance
comic book/comic strip
comic opera
coming-of-age (n.)
coming-out (n.)
commingle: Blend together; mix.
common law
common-law marriage

29

commonplace
common sense (n.)
commonsense (adj.)
common stock
commonweal/
    commonwealth
companion piece
companionway (Nautical)
compos mentis (L.)
computerized axial
    tomography (CAT)
computer literacy
computer-literate (adj.)
comrade in arms
Comsat™ (Satellite
    Communication)
con artist
concertgoer
con game
con man
conning tower
conniption fit
consciousness-raising
consent decree
contact lens
continental shelf
contrail
control freak: One with a
    need to control his or her
    environment.
convertible bond
cookbook
cookhouse
cookie jar
cookoff (n.)
cookout (n.)
cookstove
cookware
cool-headed/
    cool-headedness
cooling degree-day
cooling-off period

coon cat/coon dog
coonhound
coon's age
coonskin
coping saw
cop-out (n.)
coppertone
copybook
copyboy
copycat (n., v., adj.)
copy desk
copyedit/copyeditor
copyholder
copy paper
copyreader
copyright
copywriter
coq au vin (F.)
cordon bleu (F.)
cordwood
core city
corkboard
corkscrew
cornball (n., adj.)
corn borer
corncake
corn chip
corncob
corncrib
cornerstone
corn-fed
cornfield
cornflakes
cornflower
cornhusk/cornhusking
cornmeal
corn muffin
corn pone (n.)
cornpone (adj.)
cornrow: Type of braid.
corn silk
cornstalk

cornstarch
cornstick
corn sugar/corn syrup
corn whiskey
corporal punishment
corps de ballet (F.)
corpus delicti (L.)
corpus juris (L.)
cost accounting
cost-effective
cost-efficient
cost of living
cost-of-living index
cost overrun
cost-plus (adj.)
cost-saving (adj.)
cost-share (v.)
cottage industry
cotter pin
cotton gin
cotton picker
cotton-picking, also
    cottonpickin' (adj.)
cottonseed oil
councilman/councilwoman
councilmember
counselor-at-law
countdown (n.)

COUNTER- WORDS
NOTE: This list doesn't pur-
port to be complete. Virtually
all the *counter*- words are
written solid.
    counteraccusation
    counteract
    counterargument
    counterattack
    counterattraction
    counterbalance
    counterblast
    counterblow

counterbore
countercharge
countercheck: Something
    that seeks to check,
    restrict, or limit.
counter check: For the
    convenience of a bank's
    customer in making
    withdrawals.
counterclaim
counterclockwise
countercoup
counterculture
countercurrent
counterforce
counterintelligence
counterirritant
countermand
countermeasure
countermine
counteroffensive
counteroffer
counterpart
counterplea
counterpoint
counterpoise
counterpose
counterproductive
counterprogramming
counterpropaganda
counterproposal
counterpunch
counterrevolution/
    counterrevolutionary
countersign
countersignature
counterstamp
counterstroke
countersue
countersuggestion
countertop
countervail

counterweight
counterwork
countrified, also
    countryfied
country-and-western (n.,
    adj.)
country-bred
country club
country cousin
country house
countryman
countrypeople
country rock
countryside
countrywide
county court
county seat
coup de grâce (F.): Death
    blow.
coup d'état (F.): Sudden
    decisive action in politics.
couples therapy
courseware (Computer
    Science)
coursework
courtesy car
court-martial (pl. courts-
    martial)
court-martialed
court of law
court of record
courtside (Sports)
courtyard
couscous: North African
    dish.
coverall(s)
cover charge
cover girl
cover-up (n.)
cowabunga: Yell of exhilara-
    tion.

cowbell
cowboy
cowcatcher (on a locomo-
    tive)
cow college
cowgirl
cowhand
cowlick: Tuft of hair.
coworker
cowpoke
cowpuncher
coxswain
crab apple
crab grass
crackdown (n.)
cracker-barrel (adj.)
crackerjack: Person or thing
    that shows remarkable
    ability.
Cracker Jack™
crackhead: Habitual user of
    crack cocaine.
crackhouse
crack of dawn
crackpot (n., adj.)
crackup (n.)
cradle-to-grave (adj.)
craftsman/craftsmanship
cram course
cram-full: Chock-full.
crankcase
crank letter
crankpin
crankshaft
crank-up (n.)
crapehanger: A pessimist.
crapshoot (n., v.)
crash course
crash dive (n.)
crash-dive (v.)
crash helmet
crash-land (v.)

crash pad
crash program
crashproof
crawlspace (n.)
crawlway
crazy bone
crazy quilt
crazyweed: Locoweed.
C-reactive protein
(Biochemistry)
cream cheese
cream of tartar
cream puff
crease-resistant
creature comforts
credit bureau
credit card
credit line
credit rating
credit union
creditworthy
creepy-crawly
crème de cacao (F.): A
liqueur.
crème de la crème (F.): The
very best.
crème de menthe (F.):
Mint-flavored liqueur.
crepe paper
crêpe suzette (F.; pl. crêpes
suzette or crêpe
suzettes): Thin dessert
pancake.
crestfallen
crew cut [Hyphenate as adj.]
crewelwork
crewman
crew neck [Hyphenate as
adj.]
cribbage board
crib death
crime-fighter

criminal code
crisis center
crisscross
crop-dust (v.)
crop duster (n.)
crop-dusting
cropland
crop out (v.)
crop up (v.)
cross-action
crossbar
crossbeam
crossbones (skull and)
cross-border (adj.)
crossbow
crossbred/crossbreed
cross-check (n., v.)
cross-claim
cross-country (n., adj.)
crosscourt (Sports)
crosscurrent
crosscut (n., v., adj.)
crosscutting (Filmmaking)
cross-dress (v.)
cross-dresser (n.)
cross-examine/
cross-examination
cross-eyed
cross-fertilization
cross-file (v.)
cross fire or crossfire (n.)
cross-grained
cross hairs
crosshatch
cross index (n.)
cross-index (v.)
cross-legged (adj.)
crossline
cross-link (v.)
cross-linkage (n.)
cross-match (v.)
cross matching (Medicine)

cross-out (n.)
crossover (n.)
cross-ownership
cross-pollinate (v.)
cross-purpose
cross-question
cross-reaction
cross reference (n.)
cross-reference (v.)
cross-resistance
crossroad
crossruff (n., v.; Bridge)
cross section [Hyphenate as adj.]
cross-section (v.)
cross-stitch
cross street
cross talk, also crosstalk: Interference on phone or radio.
cross-tolerance
crosstown (adj., adv., n.)
crosstree (Nautical)
crosswalk
crossway/crossways
crosswind
crosswise (adv., adj.)
crossword
crossword puzzle
crowbar
crowd pleaser (n.)
crowd-pleasing (adj.)
crown jewels
crown prince/crown princess
crow's-feet: Tiny wrinkles.
crow's-nest (Nautical)
cruel-hearted
cruise control
cruise missile
crumbum
crybaby

cry havoc
crystal ball
crystal-clear (adj.)
crystal gazing
cubbyhole
cube root
cube steak
cuckoo clock
cue ball (Billiards, Pool)
cue bid (n., Bridge)
cue-bid (v.)
cuff button
cuff link
cul-de-sac (F.)
culture shock
cum laude (L.)
cummerbund
cupbearer
cupcake
cupful (pl. cupfuls)
curb market
curb roof
curb service
curbside
curbstone
cure-all (n.)
curlyhead
curriculum vitae (L.)
currycomb
curry powder
curse word
curtain call
curtain raiser
curtain time
curtain wall
curve ball
cussword
custom-built
custom-made
cut-and-dried (adj.)
cut-and-paste (adj.)
cutaway (Tailoring)

cutback (n.)
cutdown (n., adj.)
cutie pie/cutesy pie
cut-in (n., Motion Pictures, etc.)
cutoff (n., adj.)
cutout (n.)
cutover (adj., n.)
cutpurse
cut rate [Hyphenate as adj.]
cutthroat
cutting board
cutting edge
cutting room
cutup (n.)
cutwater (Nautical)
cutwork
cyberpunk: A computer hacker.
cyberspace

D

dad-blamed/dad-blasted: Mild oaths.
daily bread
daily double
dairy cattle
dairy farm
dairyland
dairyman
daisy chain
daisy wheel
damfool (n., adj.)
damp-mop (v.)
dampproof (adj., v.)
damyankee
dance band
dance hall
dance of death
dapple-gray

daredevil
daresay (v.)
Dark Ages
dark-eyed
dark horse
dark meat
dark of the moon
darkroom
dart board
dashboard
data bank
database
datacenter
data highway (n.): Information superhighway.
data processing
datebook
dateline
date of record
date rape
date stamp (n.)
date-stamp (v.)
daughter-in-law (pl. daughters-in-law)
daybed
daybook
daybreak
day-by-day (adj.)
day care [Hyphenate as adj.]
day coach
daydream (n., v.)
Day-Glo™: Used for fluorescent materials or colors.
dayglow: Airglow seen during the day.
day in court
day in, day out
day labor/day laborer
day letter
daylight saving
daylong (adj.)

day nursery
Day of Atonement
day one
daypack
day room
day school
day shift
daytime
day-to-day (adj.)
day-trip (v.)
day-tripper (n.)
daywear
daywork
deaccession (n.): Selling a work of art from a museum.
dead air
dead-air space
deadbeat
dead bolt
dead center
dead duck
dead end (n.)
dead-end (adj., v.)
deadeye (Nautical)
deadhead
dead heat
dead horse
dead letter
deadlight (Nautical)
deadline
dead load
deadlock
deadman (Building Trades; Nautical)
dead-man's float (Swimming)
dead-on (adj.): Exactly right.
deadpan
dead-reckon (v.)
dead reckoning (n.)
dead ringer

dead run
dead set
dead space
dead storage
dead water
dead weight
deadwood
deaf-and-dumb (adj.)
deaf-mute
dealmaker
Dear John (letter)
deathbed
death benefit
deathblow
death camp
death chamber
death mask
death rate
death row
death sentence
death's-head
deathtrap
deathwatch
death wish
debt limit
debug
debunk
decaf (n., adj.): Decaffeinated coffee or tea.
decathlon
decay time (Physics)
decision-maker/ decision-making
deck chair
deck hand
deckhouse (Nautical)
deckle edge (n.)
deckle-edged (adj.)
deejay
deep-chested (adj.)
deep-dish (adj.)

deep-dyed (adj.)
deep fat
deep freeze (n.)
deep-freeze (v.)
deep freezer (n.)
deep fryer
deep-laid (adj.)
deep pocket(s)
deep-rooted (adj.)
deep-sea (adj.)
deep-seated (adj.)
deep-set (adj.)
deep six (n.): Burial at sea.
deep-six (v.)
Deep South
deep-voiced (adj.)
deepwater (adj.)
deerskin
deerstalker: A hat.
de-escalate
de-excite (Physics)
de facto (L.)
defame
defang
defocus (v., n.)
defog (v.)
defogger (n.)
degree-day (n.)
deice (v.)
deicer (n.)
déjà vu (F.)
de jure (L.)
delayed action [Hyphenate as adj.]
delimit
delist
delouse
delta ray
delta rhythm
delta V
deluxe (adj., adv.)
demigod

demimonde (F.): Prostitutes or courtesans.
demitasse
démodé (F): Out of date.
den mother
de novo (L.)
Denver boot
depth charge
de rigueur (F.): Required by custom or etiquette.
dernier cri (F.): The latest fashion.
derring-do: Daring deeds.
desert rat
desex
deskbound
deskman
desktop publishing
detail man
detox (n.)
de trop (F.): Too much; superfluous.
deus ex machina (L.): An artificial device resolving problems in the plot.
deutsche mark (G.)
devil-may-care (adj.)
devil's food cake
dewclaw
dewlap
dew point
dewy-eyed (adj.)
dial tone
dial-up (adj., Computers)
diamond ring effect (Astronomy)
diaper rash
diddly-squat: "It isn't worth diddly-squat."
die cast (v.)
die-cast (adj.)
die casting (n.)

die-hard (adj.)
die-off (n.)
diet kitchen
diet pill
dill pickle
dillydally
dimbulb: Dimwit.
dimout (n.)
dimwit (n.)
dimwitted
diner-out (pl. diners-out)
ding-a-ling
dingbat
dingdong (n., adj.)
dining room
dinner dance
dinner dress
dinner jacket
dinner ring
dinnertime
dinnerware
diplomatic corps
dipstick
dipsy-doodle
direct-access (adj., Computers)
direct current
direct deposit
direct distance dialing
directed verdict
direct evidence
direct examination
direction finder
direct mail [Hyphenate as adj.]
direct-mailer
direct tax
dirt bike
dirt-cheap (adj., adv.)
dirt farm/dirt farmer
dirt poor
dirt road

dirty bomb
dirty linen
dirty-minded
dirty old man
dirty pool
dirty tricks
dirty war
dirty word
dirty work
disc brake
disc jockey
discount broker
discount house
discount rate
discount store
dishcloth
dishpan hands
dishrag
dishtowel
dishware
dishwasher
dishwasherproof
dishwater
disk drive (Computer Science)
disk harrow
disorderly conduct
display ad
distress call
district attorney
disuse
ditchdigger
ditchwater
ditto mark
ditty bag
dive-bomb (v.)
dive bomber/dive bombing
diving board
diving suit
divining rod
divorcé (F., man)
divorcée (F., woman)

divvy up
Dixie Cup™
Dixieland
doable
do-all (n.)
dockhand
docking station
dockside
dockwalloper
dockworker
dockyard
docudrama
dodo: Extinct bird; stupid person.
doeskin
dog and pony show
dog biscuit
dogcart
dogcatcher
dog collar
dog days
dog-doo
dogear (n., v.)
dog-eared (adj.)
dog-eat-dog (adj.)
dogface
dogfight
doggy bag
doghouse
dog in the manger
dogleg (n., adj., v.)
dog-legged (adj.)
dognap
do-good (adj.)
do-gooder
dog paddle
dog's breakfast
dog show
dogsled
dog tag
dog-tired
dogtrot

dog-walker
dogwatch (Nautical)
do-it-yourself (adj.)
do-it-yourselfer
dolce vita (It.): Sweet life.
dollar-a-year man
dollar day [Hyphenate as adj.]
dollar diplomacy
dollars-and-cents (adj.)
dollar sign
dollarwise (adj.)
dolled up (adj.)
dollface
dollhouse
doll up (v.)
domino effect
domino theory
done deal
Don Juan
donkey's years
donkeywork: Drudgery.
donnybrook
donor card
do-nothing (n., adj.)
do-nothingism
don't-know (n.): Person with no opinion (in a poll, e.g.).
doodad
doodlebug
doohickey
doomsayer
doomsday
doorbell
door check
do-or-die (adj.)
doorjamb
doorkeeper
doorknob
doorman
doornail (dead as a)
door opener

door prize
doorstep
doorstop
door-to-door (adj., adv.)
doorway
dooryard
dope addict
doped-out (adj.)
dope fiend
dopehead
dope pusher
dopesheet
doppelgänger (G.)
Doppler effect (Physics)
dorsal fin
dos and don'ts
dose-response curve
do-si-do: Square-dance
   figure.
double-acting (adj.)
double-action (adj.)
double agent
double-barreled
double bed
double-bill (v.)
double bind (Psychology)
double-blind (experiment)
double boiler
double-breasted
double check (n.)
double-check (v.)
double-crop (v.)
double cross (n.)
double-cross (v.)
Double-Crostic™: A puzzle.
double-cut (adj.)
double date (n.)
double-date (v.)
double-deal/double-dealing
double-deck (adj.)
double-decker (n.)
double-digit (adj.)

double dip (n.)
double-dip (v., adj.)
double-dipping (n.)
double dribble (Basketball)
double-duty (adj.)
double-edged (adj.)
double-ended (adj.)
double entendre (F.)
double-entry (adj.,
   Bookkeeping)
double exposure
   (Photography)
double-faced (adj.)
double fault (Tennis)
double feature
doubleheader
double helix
double-hung (adj.)
double indemnity
double jeopardy
double-jointed (adj.)
double-knit (n., adj.)
double-lock (v.)
double negative (Grammar)
double occupancy
double-park (v.)
double play (Baseball)
double-quick (adj., adv.)
double-ring (ceremony)
double-space (v.)
doublespeak (n.)
double standard
double take (n.)
double-talk (n., v.)
doublethink
double time (n.)
double-time (v.)
double up (v.)
double vision
double-wide (adj.)
double wingback
   formation (Football)

douche bag
dough box
doughboy
dovetail
dowager's hump
Dow Jones Average™
down-and-out (adj.)
down-and-outer (n.)
down-at-the-heel(s) (adj.)
downbeat
down-bow (Music)
downcast
downcourt (as in basketball)
downdraft
down east or Down East
down-easter or
    Down-Easter
downfall
downfield (adj., adv.)
downgrade
downhaul (Nautical)
downhearted
downhill
down-home (adj.)
download (Computers)
down payment
downplay
downpour
downrange (adv., adj.)
downrate (v.)
downright
downriver
downscale (adj., v.)
downshift
downside
downsize (v., adj.)
downsizing (n.)
downslide
downspin
downspout
downstage
downstairs

downstate
downstream
downstroke
downswing
Down syndrome, also
    Down's syndrome
downtake
down-the-line (adj., adv.)
downtick
downtime
down-to-earth (adj.)
downtown
downtrend
downtrodden
downturn
down under (Australia, New
    Zealand)
downward
downwash
downwind
downzone (v.)
draft beer
draft board
draft dodger
draftsman
draggletail (n.)
draggle-tailed (adj.)
dragline
dragnet
drag race
drainpipe
drainspout
dramshop
drawback
drawbar
drawbridge
drawdown (n.)
drawhole (Mining)
drawing account
drawing board
drawing room [Hyphenate
    as adj.]

41

drawing table
drawknife
draw poker
drawsheet
draw shot (Billiards, Pool)
drawstring
dreadlocks
dreadnought
dreamboat
dreamland
dream team
dream world
dress circle
dress code
dress down (v.)
dress goods
dressing-down: Severe reprimand.
dressing gown
dressmaker
dress rehearsal
dress shirt
dress up (v.)
dress-up (adj.)
dribs and drabs
dried-up (adj.)
driftwood
drill chuck
drillmaster
drill press
drill team
drill tower
drip coffee
drip-dry (n., v., adj., adv.)
drip feed (n.)
drip-feed (v.)
drip pan
driveaway (n., Automotive)
drive-by (n., adj.)
drive-in (n., adj.)
driveline
driver ed

drive shaft
drivethrough (n., adj.)
drive train
drive-up (adj.)
driveway
driving iron (Golf)
driving range (Golf)
driving time
dropback (n.): Lowering of prices.
drop cloth
drop curtain
drop-dead (adj.)
drop forge (n.)
drop-forge (v.)
drop-in (n., adj.)
drop kick (n., Football)
drop-kick (v.)
drop leaf [Hyphenate as adj.]
drop letter
droplight
dropline (Journalism)
drop-off (n., adj.)
dropout (n.)
drop pass (Hockey, Soccer)
dropped seat
dropped waist
drop seat
drop-ship (v.)
drop shipment/
    drop shipper
drop shot (Sports)
drop siding
dropsonde (Meteorology)
drop valve
drop window
drop zone
drownproof/drownproofing
drug abuse
drug addict
drugged-out (adj.)

drugmaker
drugpusher
drugstore
drum and bugle corps
drumbeat/drumbeater
drum brake
drum corps
drumhead (n., adj.)
drum major/drum
   majorette
drumroll
drumstick
drunk driving
dry-as-dust (adj.)
dry battery
drybrush (n., Drawing or
   Painting)
dry cell
dry-clean (v.)
dry cleaner/dry cleaning
dry dock (n.)
dry-dock (v.)
dry eye
dry-eyed (adj.)
dry fly (Angling)
dry goods
dry-gulch (v.)
dry hole
dry ice
drying-out (n.)
dry kiln
dry law
dry measure
dry nurse (n.)
dry-nurse (v.)
dryout (n.)
dry plate
drypoint (Engraving)
dry-roasted
dry rot
dry run
dry-salt (v.)

dry-shod
dry sink
dry spell
dry wall (Building Trades)
dry wash (n.)
dry well
d.t.'s: Delirium tremens.
dual citizen
dual-purpose (adj.)
duckboard
duck-footed
duck hawk
duckpin (Bowling)
duck soup
ducktail
duckwalk
ductwork
dude ranch
due bill
dues-paying (adj., n.)
dullsville
dull-witted
dumbbell
dumb bid
dumb bunny
dumb cluck
dumb down (v.): To rewrite
   for a less intelligent audi-
   ence.
dumbfound, also dumfound
dumb show
dumbstruck
dumbwaiter
dumdum: Bullet.
dum-dum: Stupid person.
dummkopf (G.): Stupid
   person.
dumpcart
dumping-ground
dumpsite
Dumpster™
dump truck

dunce cap
dunderhead
dune buggy (n.)
dune-buggy (v.)
dunghill
dunk shot (Basketball)
duodecimal
dura mater
dust ball
dust-bathe
dustbin
Dust Bowl
dustcloth
dust cover
dust devil
dustheap
dust mop (n.)
dust-mop (v.)
dustoff (Military slang)
dustpan
dustproof
dust ruffle
dust storm
dustup: Quarrel.
Dutch courage
Dutch treat
Dutch uncle
duty-free
dwarf star
dwelling house/dwelling
   place
dyed-in-the-wool
dyestuff
dysfunction

E

eager beaver
eagle eye
eagle-eyed (adj.)
Eagle Scout

earache
eardrop: An earring.
ear drops: Medicine.
eardrum
earflap
earful
earlap
early bird
early on
early-warning system
earmark
earmuff
earned income
earned run
earnest money (Law)
earphone
earpiece
ear-piercing (adj.)
earplug
earshot
earsplitting
ear tag
earthbound
earthenware
earth-god/earth-goddess
earthlight
earthman
earth mother
earthmover
earthmoving
earthrise
earthshaking
earth-shattering
earthshine
earthstar
earth station
earth tone
earthward/earthwards
earthwoman
earthwork
earwax
earwig

earwitness
eastbound
east coast
Eastern Standard Time
east-northeast
east-southeast
eastward
easy-care (adj.)
easy chair
easygoing
easy listening
easy mark
easy money
easy street
eau de cologne (F.)
eau de vie (F.)
eavesdrop
ebb tide
echocardiogram/
   echocardiograph
echo chamber
echo check (Computer
   Science)
economy class [Hyphenate
   as adj.]
economy-size (adj.)
ecosphere
ecosystem
eddy current
edge-grain/edge-grained
edge tool
edgeways
edgewise
editor in chief
eggbeater
egg case
egg cell
egg coal
eggcrate
egg drop soup
egg foo yung
egghead (n.)

eggheaded
eggnog
egg roll
eggshell (n., adj.)
egg timer
egg tooth
egg white
ego trip (n.)
ego-trip (v.)
eightball
eightfold
eighty-niner
eighty-six (v.): To refuse to
   serve (a customer); to dis-
   card, reject (slang).
either-or
eke out
elbow-bender
elbow grease
elbowroom
el cheapo (slang)
Elderhostel™
electric eye
electric field
electronic mail
electroshock
eleventh hour
E-mail (sometimes e-mail)
emcee (n., v.)
emery board
eminent domain
empty calorie
empty-handed
empty-headed
empty nest
empty nester
empty nest syndrome
en banc (F.): By the whole
   court.
en bloc (F.): As a whole.
en brochette (F.): On a
   skewer.

encounter group
end-all (n.): Ultimate object.
end around (Football)
end game
endgate
end line (Sports)
end man
end mill
endmost
endnote
end-of-file (Computers)
end paper
end plate (Mining)
endplay (n., v.; Bridge)
end point (sometimes endpoint — consult dictionary)
end product
end run (Football)
end table
end use/end user
endways
endwise
end zone (Football)
enfant terrible (F.)
en gros (F.): Total; whole-sale.
en masse (F.): All together; as a group.
en passant (F.): In passing.
en route (F.)
entranceway
entry blank
entry-level (adj.)
entryway
envoy extraordinary
epicenter
epoch-making
Epsom salt(s)
Epstein-Barr virus
equal opportunity
[Hyphenate as adj.]

Erector Set™
erenow
errand boy
error of closure (Surveying)
erstwhile
escape artist
escape clause
escape hatch
esprit de corps (F.)
estate tax
et al. (L.): Abbreviation of et alii (and other people) or et alia (and other things).
et cetera
et ceteras: A number of other unspecified persons or things.
et seq. (L.): Abbreviation of et sequens (and the fol-lowing).
et tu, Brute (L.): And thou, Brutus.
et ux. (L.): And wife.
evenhanded
evening dress/evening gown
evening star
evening watch
eveningwear
even-minded
even money
evensong
even-steven
even-tempered
everbearing
everblooming
evergreen
everlasting
everyday (adj.): "We wear our everyday clothes every day but Sunday."
everyone (pron.): "Everyone

must go, and that means every one of you."

everyplace (adv.) "We looked everyplace for it." [Note: Write as two words when preceded by a preposition.]

everyway (adv.): "They tried everyway to help, in every way they could."

every which way

evildoer

evil eye

evil-minded

NOTE: When the prefix *ex-* denotes former, hyphenate: *ex-president, ex-child actor, ex-wife.*

ex cathedra (L.): From the seat of authority.

ex curia (L.): Out of court.

exit poll

ex parte (L.)

ex post facto (L.)

express lane

ex rights (Stock Exchange)

extra-base hit

extracurricular

extragalactic

extrajudicial

extralateral (Mining)

extralegal

extramarital

extrasensory

extrasolar

extraterrestrial

extraterritorial

extrauterine pregnancy

extravehicular

exurb

exurban/exurbanite

exurbia

eye appeal

eyeball-to-eyeball

eye bank

eyebar (Civil Engineering)

eyebath

eyebeam

eyebolt

eye-catcher

eye-catching

eye chart

eye contact

eye doctor

eyedropper

eye drops

eye-filling

eyeful

eyeglass

eyeground

eyehole

eyelift

eyeliner

eyeopener

eye-opening

eyepiece

eye-popper

eye-popping (adj.)

eye rhyme

eyeservice: Work done only when the boss is watching.

eyeshade

eye shadow

eyeshot

eyesight

eye socket

eyes-only (adj.)

eyesore

eyestrain

eyetooth

eyewash

eyewitness

F

face card
facecloth
facedown (n., adv.)
face-harden
face-lift
face mask
face-off (Ice Hockey)
faceplate
face powder
face-saver (n.)
face-saving (adj.)
face-to-face
faceup (adv.): With the face up.
face value
fact finder
fact-finding (n., adj.)
fact(s) of life
factory outlet
fadeaway (n.)
fade-in (Movies, TV)
fade-out (Movies, TV)
fag end
fail-safe (adj., n., v.)
faintheart (n.)
fainthearted (adj.)
fair ball
fair catch (Football)
fair game
fairground
fair-haired
fairlead (Nautical)
fair market price
fair market value
fair-minded
fair play
fair shake
fair territory
fair to middling

fair trade (n.)
fair-trade (adj., v.)
fair-trade agreement
fairway
fair-weather (adj.)
fairy tale [Hyphenate as adj.]
fait accompli (F.; pl. faits accomplis): Accomplished fact(s).
faith healing
fallback (n., adj.)
fall guy
falling-out
falloff (n.)
fallout (n.)
false alarm
false arrest
false bottom
false card (n., Bridge)
false-card (v.)
false colors
false dawn
false front
false-hearted
false horizon
false labor
false move
false pretense
false start (n.)
false-start (v., Sports)
false step
falsework (Construction)
family circle
family leave
family man
family style (n., adj.)
family way: Pregnant.
fan belt
fan club
fancy dress
fancy-free (adj.)

fancy man
fancy up (v.)
fancywork
fandango (Dance)
fanfare
fanfold
fanjet
fan letter/fan mail
fanlight
Fannie Mae (FNMA: Securities)
fantail
fan-tan: Card game.
fantasyland
fanwise (adv.)
far and wide (adv.)
faraway (adj.)
farebox
fare card
fare-thee-well (n.)
far-fetched (adj.)
far-flung (adj.)
far-gone (adj.)
farm belt
farm hand
farmhouse
farmland
farmout (n.)
farmworker
farmyard
far-off (adj.)
far-out (adj.)
far-point (Ophthalmology)
far-reaching (adj.)
far-red (adj.; radiation wavelengths)
farseeing
farsighted
fashion plate
fast and loose (adv.)
fastback (Automobile)
fastball (Baseball)

fast break (n., Basketball)
fast-break (v.)
fast-breaking
fast-breeder reactor
fast buck
fast day
fast food [Hyphenate as adj.]
fast-forward (n., v.)
fast lane
fast motion
fast-moving (adj.)
fast-talk (v.)
fast time
fast track (n.)
fast-track (v., adj.)
fast worker
fatback
fat body (Entomology)
fat cat
fat farm
fathead
fatheaded
father confessor
father figure
father image
father-in-law (pl. fathers-in-law)
fat lip
fatso
fat-witted
faultfinder/faultfinding
fault line
faux pas (F., sing. and pl.)
favorite son
fax modem
feather bed (n.)
featherbed (v.)
featherbedding
featherbrain
feathercut
feather duster

featherstitch
featherweight
feature-length (adj.)
feature story
FedEx
fed up (adj.)
feeble-minded
feedback
feedbag
feedbox
feedlot
feedstock
feedstuff
feedthrough (Electronics)
feedwater
fee simple
fee-splitting
feetfirst (adv.)
feet of clay
fellow creature
fellowman
fellowship
fellow traveler
felt-tip pen
femme fatale (F.)
fence-mending
fence-sitter/fence-sitting
fender bender
Ferris wheel
ferryboat
fetlock
fever blister
fever pitch
fiberboard
Fiberglas™: A brand of fiberglass.
fiberglass (n., v.)
fiber optics
fickle-minded
fiddleback (n., adj.)
fiddle bow
fiddle-de-dee

fiddle-faddle
fiddlesticks
field corn
field day
fielder's choice (Baseball)
field goal (Football)
field grade (Military)
field marshal
fieldstone
field-strip (v.)
field-test (v.)
field trip
fieldwork
field-worker
FIFO: First-in, first-out.
fifth column
fifth wheel
fifty-fifty
fighter-bomber
fighting chance
fig leaf
figure eight
figurehead
figure of speech
figure skater/figure skating
file card
file clerk
filename
file-server
filet mignon
fill-in (n.)
film clip
filmmaker/filmmaking
film noir (F.)
filmscript
filmset/filmsetter/
    filmsetting
filmstrip
filter tip
filthy lucre
finance charge
finback (whale)

finder's fee
fine art(s)
fine-comb (v.)
fine-cut (adj.)
fine-drawn (adj.)
fine-grain (adj.)
fine-grained (adj.)
fine print
fines herbes (F.)
finespun (adj.)
fine-tooth comb
fine-tune (v.)
fingerboard (Music)
finger bowl
fingerbreadth (n.)
finger food
finger hole
finger man
fingermark
fingernail
finger-paint (v.)
finger painting (n.)
finger-pointing
fingerprint
fingertip
finishing school
finishing touch
finish line
fink out (v., slang)
fire alarm
fire-and-brimstone (adj.)
firearm
fireball
firebase (Military)
fireboat
firebomb (n., v.)
firebox
firebrand
firebreak
firebrick
fire brigade
firebug

fire chief
fire clay
fire control
firecracker
firedamp (Mining)
fire door
fire drill
fire-eater
fire engine
fire escape
firefight: An exchange of
    gunfire.
firefighter
fireflood (Oil Drilling)
fireguard
fire hose
firehouse
fire hydrant
fire irons
firepan
fireplug
firepower
fireproof
fire sale
fire screen
fireside
fire station
firestop
firestorm
firetrap
fire truck
fire wall
firewarden
firewater
firewood
firework(s)
firing line
firing pin
firing squad
first aid [Hyphenate as adj.]
first base
first blood

firstborn (n., adj.)
first class [Hyphenate as adj. or adv.]
first-come (adj.)
firstcomer
first cousin
first-day cover (Philately)
first-degree (adj.)
first down (Football)
first edition
first family
first generation [Hyphenate as adj.]
firsthand (adj., adv.)
first mate
first name (n.)
first-name (adj., v.)
first night
first-nighter
first offender
first person [Hyphenate as adj.]
first-rate (adj., adv.)
first strike
first-string (adj.)
first-termer
first-time (adj.)
first-timer
first water
fiscal year
fish and chips
fishbowl
fish cake
fisheye (n., adj.)
fisheye lens (Photography)
fish farm
fish fry
fishhook
fishing banks
fishing expedition
fishing ground
fishing pole/fishing rod

fishkill
fish ladder
fish meal
fishmonger
fishnet
fishplate
fishpond
fishpound
fishskin: A condom.
fish stick
fish story
fishtail
fishtank
fishwife
fistfight
fistful
fisticuff(s)
fitting room
five-and-dime (n., adj.)
five-and-ten (n., adj.)
five-by-five: Short and fat (slang).
five o'clock shadow
five-speed (n., adj.)
five-spot
five-star (adj.)
fixed bridge (Dentistry)
fixed charge
fixed cost
fixed-income (adj.)
fixed-length (adj., Computers)
fixed-point (adj.)
fixed price
fixed star
fixer-upper (n.)
fix-it (adj.)
fizzwater
flabbergast (v.)
flagpole
flagship
flagstaff

flagstick
flagstone
flag stop
flag-waver/flag-waving
flake out (v.): Take a nap.
flak jacket
flame-out (n., Aeronautics)
flameproof
flame retardant [Hyphenate as adj.]
flamethrower
flannelboard
flannelmouth
flapdoodle: Nonsense.
flap door
flapjack
flareback (n.)
flare-up
flashback
flashboard
flashbulb
flash burn
flashcard or flash card
flashcube
flash flood
flash-forward (Motion Pictures)
flashgun
flash in the pan
flash lamp
flashlight
flashover (n., v.)
flash point
flashtube
flatbed
flatcar (Railroad)
flatfoot/flatfeet
flat-footed (adj.)
flatiron
flat-knit (adj.)
flatland
flat out (adv.)

flat-out (adj.): "He said flat out it was a flat-out lie."
flattop
flatware
flatwork (n., laundry)
flaxseed
fleabag
fleabite
flea-bitten
flea collar
flea market
fleet-footed
flesh and blood
flesh color
flesh peddler
fleshpot
flesh wound
fleur-de-lis (F.; pl. fleurs-de-lis)
flextime
flibbertigibbet
flight attendant
flight bag
flight control
flight deck
flight line
flight path
flight pay
flight plan
flight recorder
flight strip
flight-test (v.)
flightworthy
flimflam (n., v.)
flint glass
flintlock
flip chart
flip-flop (n., v.)
flip side
flip-top
flip-up (adj., v.)
float bridge

floating dock
floating-point (adj.)
floating rib
floating stock
float valve
flood control
floodgate
floodlight
floodplain
flood tide
flood wall
floodwater
floodway
floorboard
floorcover
floor lamp
floor-length (adj.)
floor manager
floor model
floor sample
floor show
floor trader
floorwalker
flophouse
flopover (TV problem)
floppy disk
flowback (n.)
flow chart (n.)
flow-chart (v.)
flower child
flower girl
flowerpot
flowmeter
flowstone
flubdub
flue pipe
flue stop (Music)
fluid drive
fluid ounce
flush-deck (adj., Nautical)
flutterboard
flutter kick (Sports)

flux gate
flyaway (adj.)
flyback (Electronics)
fly ball (Baseball)
flyblown
flyboy
flyby (pl. flybys)
fly-by-night (adj.)
fly-cast (v.)
fly-casting
fly-fishing
fly front (n.)
fly-in (n., adj.)
flyleaf
flyoff (n.)
flyover (n.)
flypaper
flypast (n.)
fly rod
fly sheet
flyspeck
fly-up (n.)
flyweight (n., Boxing)
flywheel
focal length
focal point
focus group
fog bank
fogbound
foghorn
fog light
foldaway (adj., n.): A bed,
    e.g.
fold-down (adj.)
foldout (n., adj.)
foldup (n.)
folk art
folk dance
folklore
folk music
folk singer/folk singing
folk song

follow-on (adj.)
follow-through (n.)
follow-up (n., adj.)
foodaholic
food bank
food chain
food-gathering (adj.)
food poisoning
food processor
food stamp
foodstuff
foolhardy
foolproof
foolscap
foot-and-mouth disease
footbath
footboard
foot brake
footbridge
footcare
foot-dragging
footfall
foot fault (Tennis)
footgear
foothill
foothold
foot-in-mouth disease
  (facetious)
footlights
footlocker
footlong
footloose
footmark
footnote
footpad
footpath
footplate
foot-pound/foot-poundal
  (Physics)
footprint
footrace
foot rail

footrest
footscraper
footsore
footstep
footstool
footwall
foot warmer
footwear
footwork
forasmuch as
forced-draft (adj.)
forced march
force-draft (v.)
force-feed/force-fed
force majeure (F.; pl. forces
  majeures)
force of habit
force-out (n., Baseball)
force play (Basketball)
fore-and-aft (adj., adv.)
fore-and-after (n.): A sailing
  vessel.
forearm
forebear(s): Ancestor(s).
forebode (v.)
foreboding (n.)
forebrain
forecastle deck
fore-check (Hockey)
forecourt (Tennis)
foredeck
foredoom
forefather
forefinger
forefoot
forefront
foregather
foreglimpse
forego/forewent/foregone/
  foregoing: Precede (etc.).
  [Compare with *forgo*.]
foregone conclusion

foreground
forehand/forehanded
foreign-born
forejudge
foreknowledge
forelady
foreleg
forelimb
forelock
foreman/foreperson
foremast (Nautical)
forepart
foreplay
forequarter
forerunner
foresail
foresee
foreshadow
foreshock (Geology)
foreshorten
foresight
foreskin
forestall
foretaste
foretell
forethought
foretopman (Nautical)
foretopmast
foretopsail
forevermore
forewarn
forewoman
foreword: Short introductory statement in a book.
forgo/forwent/forgone/forgoing: Abstain, etc.
for-instance (n.): "Here's a for-instance of my plan."
forklift
formfitting
form letter
for-profit (adj.)

forsake
forswear/forsworn
forthcoming
forthright
forthwith
fortnight/fortnightly
fortune cookie
fortune hunter
fortuneteller/fortunetelling
forty-niner
forty winks
forward-looking
forward pass
fossil fuel
foster care
foster child
fouled-up (adj.)
foul line (Baseball)
foulmouthed
foul play (n.)
foul shot (Basketball)
foul tip (Baseball)
foul-up (n.)
founding fathers (often capped)
fountainhead
four-bagger (Baseball)
four-ball (adj., Golf)
four bits
four-channel (adj.)
four-dimensional
four flush (Poker)
four-flush (v.)
four-flusher (n.)
fourfold
four-footed
four freedoms
four-handed
four-hundred-day clock
four-in-hand: Necktie.
four-lane (adj., highway)
four-letter word

four of a kind (Poker)
fourposter: Bed; sailing vessel.
fourscore (and ten years ago)
foursome
four-spot: Playing card.
foursquare
four-star (adj.)
fourth-class (adj., adv.)
fourth estate
four-walling (movie distributing)
four-way (adj.)
four-wheel drive
four-wheeler
foxhole
fox trot
fraidy-cat
framepack
frameshift
frame-up
framework
freak-out (n.)
freak show
freckle-faced
free agent
free alongside ship (F.A.S.)
free and easy (adj., adv.)
freebase (v.): To purify cocaine.
freeboard (n., Nautical)
freebooter
free-bored (adj., of a rifle)
freeborn
freedom fighter
free fall (n.)
free-fall (adj., of parachutists)
free-fire zone
free-floating (adj.)
free-for-all (n., adj.)

free form [Hyphenate as adj. or adv.]
free hand (n.)
freehand (adj., adv.)
freehanded
freehearted
freehold (n., adj.; Law)
freeholder (n.)
free kick (Soccer)
freelance (n., v., adj., adv.)
freelancer
free liver [Hyphenate as adj.]
free-living (adj.)
freeload (v.)
freeloader (n.)
free love
free lunch
Freemason
freemasonry
free on board (f.o.b.)
free port
free press
free radical
free-range (adj., Farming)
free rein
free ride
free-running
free speech
free-spending (adj.)
free spirit
freestanding: Standing alone.
freestyle (Sports)
free-swinging (adj.)
freethinker
free thought
free throw lane (Basketball)
free throw line (Basketball)
free trade [Hyphenate as adj.]
free verse
freeway

free wheel (n.)
freewheel (v.)
freewheeler/freewheeling
free will (n.)
freewill (adj.): Voluntary.
freewill offering
free world
freeze-dried/freeze-dry
freeze frame (TV, Movies)
freeze-out (n.)
freezer burn
freeze-up (n.)
freezing point
free zone
freight car
freight forwarder
freight pass-through
freight train
French fries (n.)
French-fry (v.)
French kiss (n.)
French-kiss (v.)
French leave
French toast
frequent flier
fresh water (n.)
freshwater (adj.)
fret saw
fretwork
Freudian slip
fricassee (Cookery)
friction drive
friedcake
friendly fire
fringe area
fringe benefit
frog kick (Swimming)
frogman
front burner
frontcourt (Basketball)
front-drive (adj.,
   Automobile)

front-end loader
front-end processor
   (Computers)
front foot
front four (Football)
frontlash
front line (n.)
front-line (adj.)
frontlist (Publishing)
front-load (v.)
front-loaded (adj.)
front-loader/front-loading
frontman
front money
front office
front-page (adj., v.)
front rank (n.)
front-rank (adj.)
front room
front-runner
front-wheel drive
frostbite/frostbitten
frost heave
frostline
frost point
frostwork
frou-frou
frozen food
fruitcake
fruitwood
fry cook (n.)
frying pan
fuckoff (n.)
fuckup (n.)
fuddy-duddy (n., adj.)
fuel-efficient (adj.)
fuel-injected (adj.)
fullback (Football)
full-blooded (adj.)
full-blown (adj.)
full-bodied (adj.)
full-bore (adj., adv.)

full circle
full-court press (Basketball)
full-cut (Jewelry)
full dress [Hyphenate as adj.]
full-faced (adj.)
full-fashioned (adj.)
full-figured
full-fledged
full gainer (Diving)
full-grain
full-grown
full house
full-length
full-line
full moon
full-power (adj.)
full-powered
full-rigged (Sailing)
full-scale
full-service
full-size
full speed
full stop
full swing
full-term (adj.)
full tilt
full time (n.)
full-time (adj., adv.)
full-timer (n.)
fun and games
fund-raise (v.)
fund-raiser/fund-raising
funfest
funny bone
funny book
funny farm
funnyman: Comedian.
funny money
funny paper(s)
furbearer/furbearing
furbelow

furthermore
furthermost
fussbudget
fusspot
future shock
fuzzy-headed

G

gadabout
gadfly
gaff-topsail (Nautical)
gag law
gagman
gag order
gag rule
gainsay/gainsaid
gal Friday
galley proof
galley-west
gallimaufry: A hodgepodge.
gallows humor
gamecock
game fish
gamekeeper
game law
game plan
game point
gamesman
gamma ray
gandy dancer (Railroad)
gangbang
gangbuster
gangplank
gang rape (n.)
gang-rape (v.)
gangway
gap-toothed
garageman
garage sale
garbageman

gasbag
gas black
gas burner
gas chamber
gas-fired (adj.)
gas fitter
gas-guzzler
gashouse
gaslight
gasman
gas mask
gas meter
gasohol
gas station
gas tank
gasthaus (G.)
gastight
gasworks
gate-crasher
gatehouse
gatekeeper
gate leg (Furniture)
gatepost
gateway
Gatling gun
gavel-to-gavel (adj.)
gearbox
gear ratio
gearshift
gearwheel
gee whiz [Hyphenate as adj.]
gefilte fish (Jewish cookery)
Geiger counter
gemstone
gender bender
gender gap
gender-neutral (adj.)
gender-specific (adj.)
general-purpose (adj.)
generation gap
Generation X

Generation X'er
gene splicing
genetic code
gentlefolk(s)
gentleperson
gentlewoman
germfree
germproof
gerrymander
getaway (n., adj.)
get-go: Git-go.
get-out (as in all get-out)
get-together (n.)
get-tough (adj.)
getup (n.): Costume, outfit.
get-up-and-go (n.): Energy, drive.
gewgaw
ghost town
ghostwrite (v.)
ghost writer
GI Bill
gift of gab
gift tax
giftware
gift-wrap (v.)
giftwrapping
gill net (Fishing)
gill-netter
gilt-edged
gimcrack
gimlet-eyed
gin and tonic
ginger ale
gingerbread
gin mill
Ginnie Mae (GNMA: Finance)
gin rummy
girl Friday
girlfriend
GI series (Medicine)

git-go (n.): A start; beginning.
give-and-take (n.)
giveaway (n., adj.)
giveback (n.)
give-up (n.)
glad hand (n.)
glad-hand (v.)
glad rags
glamour boy/glamour girl
glamour puss
glamour stock
glare ice
glasnost (Russian)
glass block
glassblowing
glass eye
glass jaw
glassmaker/glassmaking
glassware
glassy-eyed
glee club
glide path (Aeronautics)
globetrot (v.)
globetrotter (n.)
gloom and doom
   [Hyphenate as adj.]
glory hole
glottal stop
glove compartment
glow plug
glowworm
gluepot
glue sniffing
G-man/G-men
go-ahead (n., adj.)
goal-directed
goalkeeper
goal line
goalpost
goaltender
go-around (n.)

goat cheese
gobbleygook, also
   gobbledygook
go-between (n.)
go-cart
Godalmighty (interjec.)
God-awful
godchild
goddammit
goddamn (n., adj., v.)
goddamned (adj., adv.)
goddamnedest or
   goddamndest (adj., adv.)
goddaughter
go-devil
godfather
God-fearing
godforsaken
God-given
godlike
godmother
godown: Warehouse found in
   Asia and in crossword
   puzzles.
godsend
godson
Godspeed
gofer: One who goes for
   coffee, etc.
go-getter/go-getting
goggle-eyed (adj., adv.)
go-go: Re discotheques or
   nightclubs.
go-go dancer
going-over (n.)
goings-on
goldbrick (n., v.)
goldbug
Gold Coast
gold digger
golden age/golden ager
golden handshake

golden oldie
golden parachute
golden rule
gold-filled
gold leaf [Hyphenate as adj.]
gold medal
gold mine
goldminer/goldmining
gold plate [Hyphenate as adj.]
gold-plated
gold reserve
gold rush
goldsmith
gold standard
golf bag
golf ball
golf cart
golf club
golf course
golf widow
go-no-go (adj.)
Good Book: The Bible.
good-bye (interjec.)
good cheer
good faith [Hyphenate as adj.]
good-fellowship (n.)
good-for-nothing (n., adj.)
good-hearted
good humor
good-humored
good life
good-looker (n.)
good-looking
good looks
good-natured
Good Neighbor Policy
good night: Expression of farewell.
good-night (n.): A farewell or leave-taking.

good old boy, also good ole boy
Good Samaritan
good-sized
good-tempered
good time (n., prison slang)
good-time Charlie
goodwill, also good will (n.)
goody-goody (n., adj.)
goody two shoes
goofball
goof-off (n.)
goofproof
goof-up (n.)
goo-goo
goose bumps
goose egg
goose flesh
gooseneck
goose pimples
goose step (n.)
goose-step (v.)
go-round (n.): Go-around.
go-slow (adj.)
gossipmonger
governor-general
grab bag
grab bar
grace note
grace period
grade crossing
grade point
grade school
grade-schooler
graffito (pl. graffiti)
grain of salt
grammar school
grandaunt
granddaddy
granddaughter
grande dame (F.)
grandfather clause

grandfather's clock, also
    grandfather clock
grand finale
grand juror/grand jury
grand larceny
grand mal: Severe epilepsy.
grandmother
grandnephew/grandniece
grand slam (Bridge,
    Baseball, etc.)
grandson
grandstand (n., v., adj.)
grandstand play
granduncle
graniteware
grant-in-aid
grantsmanship
grapeshot
grape sugar
grapevine
grappling iron
grasscutter
grassland
grassplot
grass roots [Hyphenate as
    adj.]
grass widow/grass widower
gravedigger
graverobber
graveside (n., adj.)
gravestone
graveyard shift
gravy boat
gravy train
graybeard (n.)
gray eminence
gray-haired
gray-headed
gray market
gray matter
greaseball
grease gun

grease monkey
greasepaint, also
    grease paint
greasy spoon
great-aunt
Great Divide
great-grandchild
great-granddaughter
great-grandfather/
    great-grandmother
great-grandparent(s)
great-grandson
greathearted (adj.)
great-nephew/great-niece
great-uncle
greenback
greenbelt
green card
green-eyed monster
greengrocer
greenhorn
greenhouse
greenhouse effect
green light
greenmail
greenroom: A lounge in a
    theater, etc., for perform-
    ers when not on stage.
greens fee
greenskeeper
green soap
greenstick fracture
green thumb
Greenwich Mean Time
griddlecake
gridiron
gridlock
grillwork
gristmill
groomsman/groomsmen
gross-out (n.)
ground ball (Baseball)

ground bass (Music)
groundbreaker/
    groundbreaking
ground-controlled
    approach (Aeronautics)
ground cover
ground crew
ground fault
groundfire
ground floor
ground fog
groundout (Baseball)
ground plan
ground plate
groundplot (n., Aeronautics)
ground rule
groundskeeper, also
    groundkeeper
groundswell
ground water
ground wave
groundwork
ground zero
groupthink
growing pains
grownup [Hyphenate as adj.]
growth fund
grubstake (n., v.)
grunt work
G-string
guard cell
guardhouse
guardian ad litem
guardrail
guardroom
guesstimate
guesswork
guesthouse
guest room
guest-shot (Radio, TV)
guest worker
guidebook

guide dog
guided missile
guideline
guidepost
guide rail
guildhall
guildsman
guilt trip
guinea pig
gum arabic
gumball/gumdrop
gumboil
gumshoe (n., v.)
gunboat
guncotton
gunfight/gunfighter
gunfire
gung ho
gunlock
gunmaker
gunmetal
gun moll
gunnysack
gunplay
gunpoint
gunpowder
gun room
gunrunner/gunrunning
gunshot
gun-shy
gunslinger
gunsmith
gunstock
gun-toting (adj.)
gunwale, also gunnel
    (Nautical)
gutbucket
gut course
gutta-percha
guttersnipe
gut-wrenching (adj.)
gyp joint

gypsy cab
gyrocompass
gyroscope

H

habit-forming
hackneyed
hacksaw
hackwork
hagridden
ha-ha (n.)
hail-fellow-well-met
  (adj., n.)
hailing distance
hailstone/hailstorm
hairball
hairbreadth: Hairsbreadth.
hairbrush
hair cell
haircloth
haircoloring
haircut
hairdo (pl. hairdos)
hairdresser/hairdressing
hairline
hair net
hairpiece
hairpin
hair-raiser (n.)
hair-raising (adj.)
hairsbreadth, also
  hair's-breadth
hair shirt
hairsplitting
hair spray
hairspring
hairstyle
hairstylist
hair trigger [Hyphenate as
  adj.]

hairweaving
hairy-faced
hale and hearty

NOTE: When in doubt,
hyphenate those nouns,
adjectives, and adverbs that
start off *half-*. Listed below
are some words that don't fall
within this "rule" or other-
wise need noting.
  half-and-half (n., adv.)
  half-assed (adj.)
  halfback (Football)
  half-baked
  half-blood: A half-breed.
  half-blooded
  half-bound
    (Bookbinding)
  half-breed
  half brother
  half-caste
  half cent
  half cock (n.)
  half-cocked
  half-cup: Half a cup.
  half deck
  half-dollar
  half-dozen
  half-duplex
  half gainer (Diving)
  half-gallon
  halfhearted
  half hitch
  half holiday
  half-hour
  half-hourly
  half-inch
  half-knot (n.)
  half-length
  half-life
  half-light

half line
half-mast
half-mile/half-miler
half-moon (n., adj.)
half nelson
half note
half pay
half-peck
halfpenny
half-pint
half-pound
half-round
half-share
half shell
half sister
half size [Hyphenate as
adj.]
half-slip
half-sole (v.)
half-staff: Half-mast.
half step (Music)
half tide
halftime
halftone (n., adj.; Art,
Printing, Photography,
etc.)
half tone (Music)
half-track
half-truth
half volley (n., Tennis)
half-volley (v.)
halfway
halfway house
half-wit/half-witted

hallmark
Halloween
hallway
halo effect
halter top
hambone (Theater)
ham-fisted

ham-handed: Clumsy.
hammer and sickle
hammer and tongs
hammerhead
hammerlock (Wrestling)
hammer mill (Mining)
hammer throw
hammertoe
hamstring (n., v.)
hand and foot (adv.)
hand and glove (adv.)
handbag
handball
handbasket
handbill
handblown (Glassware)
handbook
handbound (Books)
hand brake
handcar
hand-carry
handcart
handclap
handclasp
handcraft/handcraftman
handcuff
hand-deliver
hand drill
hand-feed (v.)
handful
hand glass
hand grenade
handgrip
handgun
hand-held
handhold
handholding
handicraft/handicraftsman
hand in glove or hand and
glove (adv.)
hand in hand (adv.)
handiwork

hand-knit
hand-launder
handlebar
handlebar moustache
hand-letter (v.)
handload (v.)
handloader (n.)
handloom
handmade
handmaid
hand-me-down (n., adj.)
hand-off (n., Football)
hand organ
handout (n.)
handover (n.)
hand over fist (adv.)
handpick (v.)
hand press
handprint
hand puppet
handrail
handrub (v.)
hand-running (adv.)
handsaw
hand screw
hands down (adv.)
hands-down (adj.)
handset (n.)
handsew/handsewn
handsfree (adj.)
handshake/handshaker
handshaking (Computers)
handshape (Sign Language)
hands-off (adj.)
hands-on (adj.)
handspring
handstand (Sports)
handstitch
hand-tailor
hand-to-hand (adj.)
hand to hand (adv.)
hand-to-mouth (adj.)

hand tool
hand truck
handwarmer
hand-wash (v.)
handweaving
handwork
handwoven
handwringing
handwrite (v.)
handwriting
handwrought
handy-andy
handy-dandy
handyman
hangdog (adj.)
hanger-on (pl. hangers-on)
hang glider/hang gliding
hangman
hangnail
hang-on (n., adj.)
hangout (n.)
hangover
hang-up (n.)
hanky-panky
hantavirus
happenstance
happi coat (Japanese)
happy dust (cocaine)
happy-go-lucky
happy hour
happy hunting ground
happy warrior
hara-kiri, also hari-kari
harbormaster
hard-and-fast (adj.)
hardback
hardball
hard-bitten
hardboard
hard-boil (v.)
hard-boiled (adj.)
hardbound (Books)

hard case [Hyphenate as adj.]
hard cash
hard copy
hard core [Hyphenate as adj.]
hardcover (Books)
hard disk (Computers)
hard-edge/hard-edged (adj.)
hard-handed
hard hat: Helmet.
hard-hat (n.): Construction worker.
hard-hat (adj.)
hardheaded
hardhearted
hard-hitting
hardihood
hard labor
hard line [Hyphenate as adj.]
hard-liner
hard news (Journalism)
hard-nosed
hard-of-hearing (adj.)
hard-on (n.)
hardpan
hard porn
hard-pressed (adj.)
hard-put (adj.)
hard rock
hard rubber
hard sauce
hardscrabble
hard sell [Hyphenate as v. or adj.]
hard-set (adj.)
hard-shell/hard-shelled (adj.)
hard stuff (Drugs)
hard-surface (adj.)
hardtack

hard-ticket (n., adj.)
hard time
hardtop
hardwall
hard water
hard-wearing
hard wheat
hard-wired (adj.)
hardwiring (Electronics, Computers)
hardwood
hardworking
harebrained
Hare Krishna
harelip
hari-kari: Hara-kiri.
hark back
harness racing
harp on (v.)
harum-scarum
harvest moon
harvesttime
Harvey Wallbanger: A cocktail.
has-been (n.)
hash browns
hash mark
hash-slinger
hasta la vista (Sp.)
hatband
hatbox
hatchback (Automobile)
hatcheck
hatchet face
hatchet job
hatchet man
hatchway (Nautical)
hat dance
hate mail
hatemonger
hat in hand (adv.)
hatpin

hatrack
hat trick (Sports)
hausfrau (G.)
haute couture (F.): High
fashion.
haute cuisine (F.): Gourmet
cooking.
have-not(s) (n.)
haw-haw: A guffaw.
hawk-eyed
hay fever
hayfield
hayfork
hayloft
haymaker
haymow
hayride
hayseed
haystack
haywire
hazardous waste
H-bomb
head and shoulders (adv.)
headband
headboard
headbox
headcheese
headcloth
head cold
head count
headdress
headfirst
headforemost
headframe
head gate
headgear
headhunt
headhunter/headhunting
headlamp
headland
headlight
headliner

headlock
headlong
headman
headmaster/headmistress
head money
headmost
headnote
head off (v.)
head-on (adj., adv.)
head over heels
headphone
headpiece
headpin (Bowling)
headquarter (v.)
headquarters (n.)
headrace
headrest
headright (Law)
headroom
headsail (Nautical)
headset
head shop (Drugs)
headshrinker
heads or tails
headspace
headspring
headstand (n., v.)
head start
headstock
headstone
headstream
headstrong
heads up [Hyphenate as
adj.]
head table
head tax
head-to-head (adj.)
headwaiter
headwaters
headway
headwind
headword

headwork
healthcare, also health care
health club
health food
hearing aid
hearing-impaired
hearsay rule
heartache
heart attack
heartbeat
heart block
heartbreak/heartbreaker
heartbreaking/heartbroken
heartburn
heart disease
heart failure
heartfelt
heart-free (adj.)
hearthside
hearthstone
heartland
heart-lung machine
heart rate
heartrending
heartsease (n.)
heartsick
heartstopper
heartstrings
heartthrob
heart-to-heart
heartwarming
heat gun
heating degree-day
heating pad
heat lamp
heat pump
heat-seal (v.)
heat shield
heatstroke
heat-treat (v.)
heat treatment
heat wave

heave-ho
heaven-sent
heavenward
heavier-than-air (adj.)
heavy-bearded
heavy-duty
heavy-footed
heavy-handed
heavy-hearted
heavy hitter
heavy-laden
heavy metal
heavyset
heavy water
heavyweight
hedgehop
hedgerow
heebie-jeebies
heehaw
heel-and-toe (adj.)
heel bone
heelplate
heigh-ho
Heimlich maneuver
heir apparent
heirloom
heir presumptive
helipad/heliport
hellbender
hellbent
hellcat
helldiver
hellfire (n.)
hell-fired (adj., adv.)
hell-for-leather (adj., adv.)
hellhole
hell-raiser
hells bells
hell week
helmsman
helping hand
helpmate

helpmeet
helter-skelter (n., adj., adv.)
he-man
hem and haw
hemistich: Half a line of
  verse.
hemstitch
henceforth
henceforward
henchman
hencoop/henhouse
hen party
henpecked
hen tracks: Scribbling.
hepcat
hereabout(s) (adv.)
hereafter
here and now: The present.
hereby
hereinabove
hereinafter/hereinbefore
hereinbelow
heretofore
hereunder
hero sandwich
hero-worship
herringbone
heyday
hide-and-seek, also
  hide-and-go-seek
hideaway
hidebound
hideout
hi-fi
higgledy-piggledy
high altar
high and dry (adv.)
high and low (adv.)
high and mighty
  [Hyphenate as adj.]
highball (n., v.)
high beam

high blood pressure
highborn
highboy
highbred
highbrow
highchair
High Church
high-class
high-colored
high comedy
high-count (adj.)
high court
high-definition (TV)
high-density (adj.)
high-end (adj.)
high-energy physics
higher-up (n.)
highfalutin or hifalutin
high fashion [Hyphenate as
  adj.]
high fidelity
high finance
high-five
highflier
high-flown
highflying
high frequency
high gear
high-grade (adj., v.)
high ground
high-handed/
  high-handedness
high-hat (adj., v.)
High Holy Day
high horse
high jinks or hijinks
high jump (n.)
high-jump (v.)
high jumper
high-key (adj.)
highland
high-level

highlife
highlight
highlighter
high liver
high-low (Poker, Bridge)
high mass (often capped)
high-minded/
  high-mindedness
high-muck-a-muck
high-necked
high noon
high-occupancy vehicle
high-octane (adj.)
high-pitched
high place (n.)
high-power/high-powered
high-pressure (v., adj.)
high-priced
high priest
high profile [Hyphenate as
  adj.]
high-proof: Whiskey, etc.
high relief
high-resolution
high-rise (adj., n.)
high-risk (adj.)
high road
high roller
high school
high sea(s)
high sign
high society
high-sounding
high-speed
high-spirited
high spirits
high-step (v.)
high-stepping (adj.)
high-sticking (Hockey)
high-strung
high style
hightail (v.)

high tech
high technology
high-tension
high-test
high-ticket (adj.)
high tide
high time
high-toned
high treason
high-up (adj., n.)
high-voltage
high water
high-water mark
highwayman
highway robbery
high wire
high-wrought
hijack (n., v.)
hijacker
hillbilly
hilltop
hindmost
hindquarter
hindsight
hinterland
hipbone
hip boot
hiphugger(s) (n., adj.)
hip joint
hip-length, also hiplength
hipline
hip-pocket (adj.)
hip roof (Architecture)
hired gun
hired hand
his-and-her (adj.)
history-making
hit-and-miss (adj.)
hit-and-run (adj.)
hitchhike/hitchhiker
hither and yon
hit list

hit man
hit-or-miss (adj.)
hit parade
hit squad
hoarfrost
hobbledehoy
hobbyhorse
hobgoblin
hobnail
hobnob
Hobson's choice
hockshop
hocus-pocus
hodgepodge
hoecake
hoedown
hogback (Geology)
hog heaven
hogshead
hog-tie (v.)
hogwash
hog-wild
ho-hum
hoi polloi
hoity-toity
hokey-pokey
holdall (n.)
holdback (n.)
hold button
holddown (n.)
holdfast (n.)
holding company (Finance)
holding pattern
holdout (n.)
holdover (n.)
holdup (n.)
hole card (Poker)
hole in one
hole-in-the-wall
holeproof
holidaymaker
holier-than-thou (adj.)

hollow-eyed
hollow leg
hollow ware or holloware
Holter monitor
holus-bolus (adv.): All at
  once.
holy bread
holy day
holy war
holy water
holy writ
home base
homebody
homebound
homeboy
home-brew
homebuilder/homebuilding
homebuyer
home-care (adj.)
home center
homecoming
home front
homegrown
home guard
homeland
homelike
homemade
homemaker/homemaking
home office
homeowner
home plate (Baseball)
home port
home range
homeroom (n.)
home rule
home run
homesick
homesite
homespun
home stand (Sports)
homesteader/homesteading
homestretch

home study
home-style
hometown
homework
homeworker
homing pigeon
Homo sapiens
honest-to-goodness
    (adj., adv.)
honeycomb
honeydew melon
honey wagon
honky-tonk (n., adj.)
honor-bound (adj.)
honor bright
honor guard
honor roll
hoodwink
hoof-and-mouth disease
hoo-ha
hook and eye
hook and ladder
hook-and-ladder company
hooked rug
hookup (n.)
hoop-de-do
hoopla
hoosegow
hootchy-kootchy
hope chest
hophead
hopped-up (adj.)
hopscotch
hop, skip and a jump
horn of plenty
horn-rimmed (adj.)
horn-rims (n.)
hornswoggle
horror story
horror-struck
hors de combat (F.): Out of
    the fight.

hors d'oeuvre (F.; pl.
    hors d'oeuvre or
    hors d'oeuvres)
horse-and-buggy (adj.)
horseback
horsecar
horsefeathers
horseflesh
horsehair
horsehide
horse latitudes
horselaugh
horse opera
horseplay
horseplayer
horsepower
horse race
horse sense
horseshoe
horse show
horse's mouth
horse's neck
horsetail
horse trade (n.)
horsetrade (v.)
horse trader/horse trading
horsewhip (n., v.)
hot air
hot bed (Metalworking)
hotbed (n., v. [in other appli-
    cations])
hot-blooded
hotbox (Railroad)
hot-button (adj.)
hot cake(s)
hotchpot (n., Law)
hotchpotch: Hodgepodge.
hot cross bun
hot-dipped
hot dog (n.)
hot-dog (v.)
hot flash

hotfoot (n., v., adj.)
hothead (n.)
hotheaded (adj.)
hothouse
hotline (n., adj.): Pertaining
  to a radio program.
hot line
hot metal (Printing)
hot money
hot pack
hot pants
hot plate
hot pot: A stew.
hot potato
hot-press (n., v.)
hot rod (n.)
hot-rod (v.)
hot seat
hotshot (n., adj.)
hot spot (n.)
hotspot (v., Forestry)
hot spring
hot stuff
hotsy-totsy
hot-tempered
hot tub
hot war
hot water [Hyphenate as
  adj.]
hot-wire (v., adj.)
hound dog
houndstooth check
  (Fabrics)
hourglass
hour hand
hourlong
house arrest
houseboat
housebound
houseboy
housebreak (v.)
housebreaker/

housebreaking
housebroken
house call
houseclean (v.)
housecleaning
housecoat
house counsel
house detective
housedress
housefront
houseguest
householder
househusband
housekeep (v.)
housekeeper/housekeeping
houselights
housemaid
housemaster
housemate
housemother
house of cards
house painter
house party
housephone
houseplant
houseraising
houseroom
house rule
housesit (v.)
house sitter
house-to-house (adj.)
housetop
house trailer
housewares
housewarming
housewife
housework/houseworker
housewrecker
hovercraft
HOV lane
how-do-you-do (n.)
howsoever

how-to (adj., n.)
hubba hubba
hubbub
hubcap
hue and cry
hugger-mugger (n., v., adj.)
hula-hula
hullabaloo
human being
human-interest story
humankind
human nature
human rights
humble pie
humdinger
humdrum
humongous
humpback (n.)
humpbacked (adj.)
humpback whale
Humpty-Dumpty
Humvee: A military vehicle.
hunchback (n.)
hunchbacked (adj.)
hundredweight
hunger strike (n.)
hunger-strike (v.)
hung jury
hungover (adj.)
hung-up
hunker down
hunky-dory
hunt and peck
hunting ground
hurdy-gurdy (n., adj.)
hurly-burly (n., adj., adv.)
hurry-scurry
hurry-up (adj.)
hush-hush (adj.)
hush money
hush puppy
hydra-headed (adj.)

hydrogen bomb
hyped-up

NOTE: All words with the prefix *hyper-* and *hypo-* are written solid. Below are some examples of these words.

hyperacidity
hyperactive/
  hyperactivity
hypercharged
hypercorrect
hypercritical
hyperextension
hyperinflation
hyperlink
hyperplasia
hypersensitive
hypersusceptible
hypertension/
  hypertensive
hyperventilate/
  hyperventilation
hypoacidity
hypoallergenic
hypochlorite
hypochondria/
  hypochondriac
hypocrite/hypocritical
hypodermic
hypoglottis
hyposensitivity
hypotensive/hypotension
hypothesis/hypothesize

I

ice age
ice bag
iceberg
iceboat/iceboater

icebound
icebox
icebreaker
icecap
ice-cold
ice cream
ice-cream cone
ice cube
icefall
ice field
ice floe
ice-free
ice hockey
icehouse
icemaker
ice pack
ice pick
ice skate (n.)
ice-skate (v.)
ice storm
ice tongs
ice-up (n.)
ice water
ID card
idée fixe (F.)
Identi-Kit™
ides of March
idiot board (TV)
idiot box (TV)
idiotproof
ill-advised
ill at ease
ill-being
ill-bred
ill-conceived
ill-considered
ill-defined
ill-equipped
ill fame
ill-fated
ill-favored
ill-fitting

ill-formed
ill-gotten
ill humor
ill-humored
ill-informed
ill-intentioned
ill-mannered
ill nature
ill-natured
illogical
ill-prepared
ill-spent
ill-starred
ill-suited
ill temper
ill-tempered
ill-timed
ill-treat (v.)
ill-use (v.)
ill will
ill-willed
ill-wisher
imagemaker
immune system
in absentia (L.)
in-and-out (adj., n.)
in-and-outer
inasmuch as
in-between (n., adj.)
inboard-outboard
inborn
inbound
inbounds (adj., Sports)
inbred
inbreed
inbreeding
in camera (Law)
in check
inchoate (adj.)
incoming (adj.)
incubus: Imaginery demon;
    nightmare.

in-depth (adj.)
Indian summer
induced drag (Aeronautics)
industrial-strength (adj.)
industrywide
indwell (v.)
indwelling (adj.)
in extenso (L.)
in extremis
infighting
in-flight (adj.)
inflow (n.)
infomercial
in forma pauperis (Law)
information highway
informercial
infra dig: Beneath one's
   dignity.
infra red
infrastructure
ingoing (adj.)
ingrained
ingrowing
ingrown (adj.)
in-house (adj., adv.)
in-joke (n.)
inkblot test
in-kind (adj.; e.g., in-kind
   relief)
inkstand/inkwell
in-law: A relative by
   marriage.
in-line (adj.)
inlying (adj.)
inner circle
inner city
inner-directed
inner ear
inner man
innermost
inner sanctum
innersole

inner space
innerspring (adj.)
inner tube
innkeeper
Inns of Court (Brit.)
inpatient
in personam (L.)
in-print (adj.)
in-process (adj.)
in propria persona (L.)
in re (L.)
in rem (L.)
inroad(s)
inrush
ins and outs
inseam
in-service (adj.)
inshore (adj., adv.)
inside job
inside loop (Aeronautics)
inside straight (Poker)
inside track
in situ (L.)
insofar as
instroke (n.)
insulin-dependent diabetes
insulin shock
intact (adj.): *Never* two
   words!
inter alia (L.)

NOTE: Words with the prefix
inter- are hyphenated only
when a proper noun or proper adjective is appended.
Below are some examples:
   interactive
   inter-American
   interborough
   interbreed
   intercellular
   interceptor

interchangeable
intercollegiate
intercontinental
interdepartmental
interdict/interdiction
interdisciplinary
inter-European
interface
interfaith
interferon
interlinear
intermarriage
International Date Line
Internet
interpersonal
interposition
interracial
interstellar
intervertebral disk

intra-abdominal (adj.)
intra-aortic (adj.)
intra-arterial (adj.)
intra-arterially (adv.)
intra-articular (adj.)
intra-atomic (adj.)

NOTE: The words listed above are the only ones we find with the prefix *intra-* that are hyphenated.

intracranial
intracutaneous
intrados (Architecture)
intragalactic
intramolecular
intramural
intranuclear
intrapreneur
intraspecies
intrauterine device

intravenous
intra vires (Law)
in utero (L.)
in vino veritas: In wine there is truth.
in vitro
in vivo
ion exchange
ironbound
ironclad
iron curtain (often capped)
iron hand
iron-handed
iron-hearted
iron lung
iron-on (adj., n.)
ironwork/ironworker
island-hop (v.)
itty-bitty, also itsy-bitsy
ivory tower
ivory-towered
ivory-white (adj.)
Ivy League

J

jabberwocky
jackanapes
jackass
jackboot/jackbooted
jackhammer
jack-in-the-box
jackknife
jackleg (adj., n.)
jack-of-all-trades
jack-o'-lantern
jackpot
jackrabbit (n., adj., v.)
jackscrew
jackstraw

jack-tar or **Jack Tar**: A sailor.
jack-up (n.)
jai alai (Sp.): Game similar to handball.
jailbait
jailbird
jailbreak
jake leg
jalapeño
jambalaya
jam-pack/jam-packed
jam session
jam-up (n.)
Jane Doe
Janus-faced
jawbone/jawboning
jawbreaker
Jaws of Life™
jaybird
Jayhawker: A Kansan.
jaywalk
Jehovah's Witness
Jekyll and Hyde
Jell-O™
jellybean
jellyfish
jelly roll
jerkwater
jerry-build (v.)
jerry-built (adj.)
Jersey barrier
jet-black
jet gun
jet lag
jetliner
jetport
jet-propelled
jet propulsion
jet set
jet stream
Jetway™
Jew's harp

jibboom (Nautical)
jiggermast (Nautical)
jigsaw puzzle
Jim Crow
jim-dandy
jimjams
jingle bells
jinrikisha
jitterbug
jiujitsu, also **jujitsu**
job bank
jobholder
job-hop (v.)
job-hopping (n.)
job-hunt (v.)
job lot
job-order costing
job-sharing
job shop
Jockey shorts™
jockstrap
Joe Blow
John Barleycorn
John Birch Society
John Bull
John Doe
John Hancock (signature)
johnnycake
Johnny-come-lately
Johnny-on-the-spot
joie de vivre (F.)
joint account
joint custody
joint stock [Hyphenate as adj.]
joint tenant
joint venture (n.)
joint-venture (v.)
jokebook
joss stick
journal box
journeyman

journeywork
joypop (v.)
joypopper
joyride
joystick
judge advocate general
judgment call
Judgment Day
judo
jug band
juiced-up
juicehead
jujitsu: Jiujutsu.
jukebox
juke joint
jumbo jet
jump ball (Basketball)
jump boot
jump cut (Movies)
jump head (Journalism)
jumping bean
jumping jack
jumping-off place
jump-off (n.)
jump rope/jumping rope
jump seat
jump-shift (Bridge)
jump shot (Basketball)
jump-start (n., v.)
jumpsuit
junction box
junglegym
junk bond
junk food
junk mail
junkman
junkyard
jury-packing
jury-rig (n., v.)
jury room
jute board

K

kaffeeklatsch
katzenjammer: Hangover.
keelhaul
keepsake
Keogh plan
kerflooey
kerflop
kerplunk
kewpie doll
keyboard
key card
key case
keyed up
keyhole
key money
keynote address
keynoter
keypad
keypunch (n., v.)
key ring
keystone
keystroke
keyword
Khmer Rouge
kibbutz: Community settlement in Israel.
kibitz (v.)
kibitzer (n.)
kickback
kick boxing
kickoff (Football)
kick plate
kick pleat
kick-start (v.)
kick starter
kiddie car
kid gloves
kidney-shaped
kidney stone

kidporn, also kiddie porn
kidskin
kid stuff
kidvid
killer bee
killer-diller
killjoy
kill shot (Sports)
kiln-dried
kilowatt-hour (n.)
kindhearted
kinfolks
king bee
kingdom come
kingfisher
kingmaker
kingpin
king-size/king-sized
kinsman/kinswoman
kiss-and-tell (adj.)
kissing cousin
kiss of death
kiss-off (n.)
kit and caboodle
kitbag, also kit bag
kitchen cabinet
kitchen police
kitchen sink [Hyphenate as
 adj.]
kitchenware
kiteflying
kith and kin
kitty-cornered [See also
 cater-corner, etc.]
Klansman
klieg light
knapsack
knee action
knee bend
kneecap
knee-deep
knee-high (adj., n.)

kneehole
knee jerk [Hyphenate as
 adj.]
knee pad
kneepan
knee pants
kneesocks
knickerbockers
knickknack
knife blade
knife-edged (adj.)
knight-errant
knighthood
knit stitch
knitwear
knockabout (n., adj.)
knockdown (n., adj.)
knock-down-drag-out (adj.)
knocked-down (adj.)
knock-kneed (adj.)
knock-knees
knockoff (n.)
knockout (n., adj.)
knothole
knotty pine
know-all (n.)
know-how
know-it-all (n.)
know-nothing (n.)
knuckle ball (Baseball)
knucklebone
knuckle down (v.)
knucklehead
knuckle joint
kowtow
KP: Kitchen police.
K ration
Ku Kluxer
Ku Klux Klan
kung fu

L

labor camp
labor force
labor-intensive
labor of love
labor pains
laborsaving
lace-curtain (adj.)
lacelike
lacemaking
lace-up (n., adj.)
lacework
lackadaisical
lackluster (n., adj.)
ladder back [Hyphenate as adj.]
ladder stitch
la-di-da
ladies-in-waiting
ladies' man, also lady's man
ladies' room
ladyfinger
lady-in-waiting
ladylike
ladylove
Lady Luck
laid-back
laissez-faire (F.)
lakefront
lakeshore
lakeside
La-La land: Hollywood.
Lally column™
lallygag (v.)
lambskin
lamb's wool
lamebrain
lame duck
lame-duck session
lampblack

lamplight
lamppost
lampshade
land bank
landfall
landfill
land-grabber
land grant
landholder/landholding
landing card
landing craft
landing field
landing gear
landlocked
landlord/landlady
landlubber
landmark
landmass (Geology)
land mine
land office
land-office business
land of Nod
landowner
land-poor
landscape architect
landslide
landsman
lantern jaw
lantern-jawed
lapboard
lap dog
lap joint (Construction)
laptop (Computers)
lares and penates: Household goods.
largehearted/ largeheartedness
large-minded/ large-mindedness
large-print (adj.)
larger-than-life (adj.)
large-scale (adj.)

laser beam
laser printer
lastborn
last-ditch (adj.)
last hurrah
last-in, first-out (LIFO)
last mile
last-minute (adj.)
last rites
last straw
last word
latchkey
latchkey child
latchstring
late bloomer
late-blooming (adj.)
late charge
latecomer
late-night (adj.)
latter-day (adj.)
Latter Day Saint: A
  Mormon.
latticework
laughing gas
laughingstock
laugh off (v.)
laugh track
launch pad
laundry list
laundryman/
  laundrywoman
law-abiding
law and order [Hyphenate
  as adj.]
law book
lawbreaker
law court
lawgiver
lawmaker
lawman
lawn mower
layabout

layaway plan
layback (Figure Skating)
lay-by (n.)
laydown (Bridge)
layer cake
lay figure
layman/layperson
layoff (n.)
lay of the land
layout (n.)
layover (n.)
lay-up (n.)
lazybones
lazy Susan
L-dopa
leadfooted
lead-free
lead glass
lead-in (n., adj.)
leading edge
leading lady/leading man
lead line (Nautical)
leadman: A worker in charge
  of other workers.
leadoff (n., adj.)
lead-out (n.)
lead-paint poisoning
lead pencil
lead-pipe cinch
lead screw
lead time
lead-up (n.)
lead white
leaf bud
leaf mold
leakproof
lean-faced
lean-to
leapfrog
leap second
leap year
learning curve

learning-disabled
leaseback
leasehold/leaseholder
lease-purchase
leash law
least common
   denominator
leastways
leastwise
leatherneck: A U.S. marine.
leatherwork
leave of absence
leave-taking
lederhosen (G.)
lee shore
lee tide
leeward
leeway
Left Bank (Paris)
left brain
left field (Baseball)
left-hand (adj.)
left-handed/left-hander
left-of-center (adj.)
leftover (n., adj.)
left wing
legal age
legal aid
legal-size (adj.)
legal tender
legerdemain: Trickery.
legman
leg-pull (n.)
legroom
leg up (n.)
legwork
leisure suit
leisurewear
leitmotif, also leitmotiv
   (Music)
lemon drop
lemon law

lend-lease
lengthways
lengthwise
lensboard
lensman
lese majesty (Law)
less-than-perfect (adj.)
let alone (conj.): To say
   nothing of.
letdown
letter bomb
letter box
letter carrier
letter drop
letterhead
letter of credit
letter-perfect (adj.)
letterpress
letter-quality
letter-size
letterspace (Printing)
letters patent
letup (n.)
levelheaded
level-off (n., Aeronautics)
level off (v.)
Levi's™
license plate
lickety-split
lie-abed (n.)
lie-by (Brit.)
lie detector
lie-in (n.)
life-and-death (adj.)
life annuity
life belt
lifeblood
lifeboat
life buoy
life cycle
life expectancy
life force

life form
life-giving
lifeguard
life history
life jacket
lifeless
lifelike
lifeline
lifelong
lifemanship
life of Riley
life-or-death (adj.)
life preserver
life raft
lifesaver
life sentence
life-size/life-sized
life span
lifestyle
life-support (adj.)
life-threatening
lifetime
lifework
LIFO: Last-in, first-out.
liftback (Automobile)
lift-drag ratio (Aeronautics)
liftgate
liftoff (n., adj.)
light-adapted
light box
light bulb
light-emitting diode
lighter-than-air (adj.)
lightface (a typeface)
lightfast
light-fingered
light-footed
light-handed
lightheaded
lighthearted
light heavyweight
lighthouse

light housekeeping
light line (Nautical)
light meter
light-minded
lightning rod
light-o'-love
light opera
lightproof
lightship
light show
lights out
light-struck (Photography)
lightweight (adj., n.)
light-year
like-minded
lily-livered
lily-white
limewater
limited-access highway
limp-wristed
linchpin
linebacker (Football)
line cut (Photoengraving)
line drive
line-haul (adj.)
line-hauler (n.)
line item
line-item veto
lineman
line of sight
line printer
line score
linesman
line space
lineup
lingua franca
linkup (n.)
linseed oil
lionhearted
lip-read (v.)
lip reading (n.)
lip service

lip-synch or **lip-sync** (v.;
  Movies, TV)
liquid air
lis pendens (Law)
listening post
list price
lit-crit: Literary criticism.
literal-minded
litmus paper
litmus test
litterbag
litterbug
littermate
little-bitty
live-action (adj.)
livebearer (Fish)
lived-in (adj.)
live-in (adj., n.)
livelong
live-out (adj.)
live steam
livetrap (n., v.)
live wire
living death
living room
living will
load fund
load-line mark (Nautical)
loadmaster
lo and behold
loan shark (n.)
loansharking
loanword
lobsterman
lobster pot
local area network
  (Computers)
lockbox
lockdown
locker room [Hyphenate as
  adj.]
lock-in (n.)

lockjaw
lock nut
lockout (n.)
locksmith
lockstep
lockup
locoweed
lodestar
lodestone
lodging house
loggerhead(s)
logjam
log line (Nautical)
logroll (v.)
logrolling (n.)
loincloth
lonely-hearts (adj.)
lone wolf
long-ago (adj.)
long arm
longboat
longbow
long distance [Hyphenate
  as adj. or adv.]
long division
long-drawn-out
long face
long-faced
long green: Paper money.
longhair (n., adj.)
longhand
long haul [Hyphenate as
  adj.]
long johns
long jump
long-lasting
long-lived
long-playing
long-range
long-run (adj.)
longshoreman
long shot

long-standing
long-stemmed
long-suffering
long suit
long-term
longtime (adj.)
long-winded
look-alike
looker-on (pl. lookers-on)
look-in: Brief glance.
looking glass
lookout (n.)
look-over (n.)
look-see
look-through (n.)
lookup (n.)
loony bin
loophole
loop-the-loop
loose cannon
loose end(s)
loose-fitting
loose-jointed
loose-leaf
loose-limbed
loose-tongued
loosey-goosey (adj.)
lop-eared
lopsided
lose-lose (as in *win-win*)
loss leader
loss ratio
lost cause
lotus-eater
lotusland
lotus position
loudmouth/loudmouthed
loudspeaker
lounge chair
lounge lizard
loungewear
love beads

lovebird
lovebug
love child
loved one
love feast
love handles
love-in (n.)
love knot
love life
lovelorn
lovemaking
love match
lovers' lane
love seat
lovesick
lovey-dovey
loving cup
loving-kindness
low-angle shot
    (Photography)
low-back (adj.)
lowball (v., n.)
low beam
low blood pressure
low blow
lowborn
lowbred
lowbrow
low-budget
low-cal
low-class
low comedy
low-cost
low-count
low country [Hyphenate as
    adj.]
low-density
low-dose (adj.)
lowdown (n.)
low-down (adj.)
low-end (adj.)
lower case (n.)

lowercase (adj., v.)
lower class [Hyphenate as adj.]
lowerclassman
Lower 48 (States)
lower house (legislature)
low frequency
low-grade
low ground
low-key
lowland(s)
lowlander
low-level
lowlife (n.)
low-minded
low-necked
low-pitched
low-power
low-pressure
low-priced
low profile
low-rate
low-resolution
low-rise (adj., n.)
low road
low-spirited
low-tar
low tech/low technology
low-tension
low-test
low-ticket
low tide
low water
low-water mark
lukewarm (adj.)
lukewarmly (adv.)
lumberjack
lumber jacket
lumberman
lumberyard
lumbosacral
lunar eclipse

lunatic fringe
lunchbox
lunch counter
lunchroom
lunchtime
lunchwagon
lusterware
lying-in (n., adj.)
Lyme disease
lymph cell
lymph gland
lymph node
lynch law
lynch mob
lynx-eyed

M

M-1: A rifle.
machine gun (n.)
machine-gun (v.)
machine-readable
machine shop
machine tool
machine-wash (v., adj.)
Machmeter
Mach number
madcap (n., adj.)
madding crowd
made-to-measure
made-to-order
made-up (adj.)
madhouse
madman/madwoman
mad money
Mae West: Life preserver.
mag card/magnetic card (Computers)
magic lantern
magna cum laude
magnum opus

maiden speech
maid of honor
maidservant
mailbag
mail bomb
mailbox
mail carrier
mail drop
Mailgram™
mailman
mail order [Hyphenate as adj.]
mail-out (n.)
mailroom
main deck (Nautical)
main drag
mainframe (Computers)
mainland
main line (n.)
mainline (v., adj.)
mainliner
mainmast (Nautical)
mainsail (Nautical)
mainsheet (Nautical)
mainspring
mainstay
main stem
mainstream (n., v., adj.)
main street
main-topgallant (Nautical)
main-topmast (Nautical)
main yard (Nautical)
maître d'/maître d'hôtel
major-domo
major league [Hyphenate as adj.]
major medical (Insurance)
make-ahead (adj.)
make-believe (n., adj.)
make believe (v.)
make-do (n., adj.)
makefast (n., Nautical)

make-or-break (adj.)
makeover (n.)
make-ready (n.)
makeshift
makeup
makeweight (n.)
makework (n.)
maladaptation
maladjusted/
maladjustment
malapropism
malapropos (adj., adv.)
mal de mer (F.):
Seasickness.
male chauvinist
malice aforethought
mama's boy
man about town
managed care
man-at-arms
man-child
man-eater
man-eating shark
manhandle
manhole cover
man-hour (n.)
manhunt
manic-depressive (adj., n.)
man in the street
man jack
Mann Act
mano a mano (Sp.): Direct confrontation.
man of letters
man of the cloth
man of the house
man of the world
man-of-war (warship)
manor house
manpower
man-sized
manslaughter

manslayer
man-tailored
mantelpiece
mantelshelf
man-to-man (adj.)
mantrap
man-year
manyfold
many-sided
maple leaf
maple sugar/maple syrup
mapmaker
marble cake
marblewood
mare's-nest
margin account
markdown
marketplace
market price
market share
market value
marksman
marksmanship
markup
marrowbone
marrowfat
marsh gas
martial law
Mary Jane: Marijuana.
mashie iron (Golf)
mashie niblick (Golf)
masked ball
masklike
Mason jar
massage parlor
mass marketing
mass media
mass murder/
    mass murderer
mass-produce (v.)
mass production
mass transit

master-at-arms
master class
master file (Computers)
master key
mastermind (n., v.)
master of ceremonies
masterpiece
master plan
master race
master's degree
masterstroke
masterwork
master workman
masthead (n., adj.)
matchboard
matchbook
matchbox
matchlist
matchlock
matchmaker
match play
match point
matchstick
matchup (n.)
materfamilias: Female head
    of household.
materia medica
matron of honor
matter of course
    [Hyphenate as adj.]
matter of fact [Hyphenate
    as adj.]
matter-of-factly (adv.)
matter of record
matzo ball
maxiskirt
Mayday: International dis-
    tress signal.
May Day: May 1st.
Maypole
mazel tov (Yid.): Good luck!
mea culpa (L.)

meadowland
meals on wheels (sometimes capped)
meal ticket
mealtime
mealy-mouthed
mean deviation
mean distance
mean solar time
meanspirited/
  meanspiritedness
meantime (n., adv.)
mean time (n.): Mean solar time.
meat and potatoes (n.): The basic or fundamental part.
meat-and-potatoes (adj.): Basic.
meat ax [Hyphenate as adj.]
meatball
meathead
meat loaf
medevac, also medivac (n., v.)
Medfly, also medfly
median strip
Medicaid
medical-legal (adj.)
Medicare
medicine dropper
medicine man
medicine show
medicolegal
meeting house

NOTE: All words with the prefix *mega-* are written solid. Some examples:
  megabit
  megabuck
  megabyte

megacycle
megadose
megahertz
megaton
megavolt
megawatt

meltdown
melting point
melting pot
meltwater
memory bank
memory lane
ménage à trois (F.)
Mendel's law
menfolk(s)
mens rea (Law): Criminal intent.
men's room
mental health
mental telepathy
mental therapy
merchant bank
merchant marine
merchant ship
merci beaucoup (F.)
mercury-vapor lamp
mercy killing
merit badge
merit system
merry-go-round
merrymaker/merrymaking
message center
mess around
mess hall
mess jacket
mess kit
messmate
mess-up (n.)
metalware
metalwork/metalworking
meter maid

meterstick
metes and bounds
methinks/methought
me-too-ism
metric system
Metroliner™
Mexican-American
mezzo-soprano
Mickey Finn
mickey mouse (adj., often
    capped)

NOTE: All words with the
prefix *micro-* are written
solid. Some examples:
    microampere
    microbiology
    microcephalic
    microchip
    microcomputer
    microcosm
    microenvironment
    microfiche
    micrograph
    microorganism
    microsecond
    microvascular
    microvolt
    microwatt

midair
midbrain
midcourse
midday
middle age (n.)
middle-aged (adj.)
Middle Ages (history)
middle-age spread
Middle America
Middle American
    [Hyphenate as adj.]
middleborn

middlebrow
middle class [Hyphenate as
    adj.]
middle distance
middle ear
Middle East
Middle English
middle ground
middleman
middle management
middle-of-the-road (adj.)
middle school
middle term
middleweight
Middle West
midfield/midfielder (Sports)
midiskirt
midland
mid-level
midlife
midlife crisis
midline (n.)
midmorning
midmost (adj., adv.)
midnight sun
midpoint
midrange
midriff
mid-rise (building)
midsection
midship
midshipman
mid-size (adj.)
midstream
midsummer
mid-teen (adj., n.)
midterm
midtown
midway (n., adj.)
midweek
midweekly (adj., adv.)
midwifery

midwinter
midyear
might-have-been (n.)
milady
mildewproof
milelong
mile-marker
milepost
milestone
military police
milk-and-water (adj.)
milk bank
milk bar
milk cow
milk glass
milk leg
milkmaid/milkman
milk run
milk shake
milksop
milk sugar
milk tooth
milk train
milk-white
Milky Way
millisecond
millpond
millrace
millstone
millstream
mill wheel
millwork
millwright
milord
milquetoast: A spineless
    person.
mincemeat
mince pie
mind-altering
mind-bending
mindblower
mind-blowing

mind-boggling
mind-expanding
mind games
mind reader/mind reading
mind-set
mind's eye
mine detector
minefield
minelayer
minesweeper
mineworker

NOTE: All standard words
with the prefix *mini-* are
written solid. Some exam-
ples:
    minibike
    minibus
    minicab
    minicomputer
    minimart
    minirecorder
    miniseries
    miniskirt

Mini-Vac™
minor key
minor league [Hyphenate
    as adj.]
minor scale
minor term
mint condition
mint julep
mintmark
minus sign
minute gun
minute hand
minuteman
minute steak
miracle man
mirror image
mirror-writing

NOTE: All words with the prefix *mis-* are written solid. Some examples:

    misadventure
    misaligned
    misanthrope
    misappropriate
    misbegotten
    misconception
    misidentify
    misquotation
    misspelling
    mistranslate

mise-en-scène (F.): Stage setting; environment.
misery index
mishmash
missile gap
missileman
missing link
misty-eyed
miter box
mitral valve
mix-and-match (adj., v.)
mixed bag
mixed grill
mixed-up (adj.)
mix-up (n.)
mizzenmast
mobile home
mobile unit
mock-heroic (n., adj.)
mock turtle soup
mock-up (n.)
modern-day (adj.)
modus operandi (L.): Mode of operating.
modus vivendi (L.): Way of life.
moldboard
molehill

moleskin
mollycoddle
Molotov cocktail
mom-and-pop (adj.)
Monday morning quarterback
money-back guarantee
moneybag(s)
money belt
moneychanger
money changing
moneygrubber
moneylender
money machine
moneymaker
moneymaking (n., adj.)
money market
money-market fund
money order
money player
money tree
monkey business
monkey jacket
monkeyshine(s)
monkey wrench
monk's cloth
monosyllabic
monotheism
mood-altering
mood music
moon-blind (adj.)
moon blindness
moonchild
moon-eyed
moon-faced
moonlight (v.)
moonlighter/moonlighting
moonprobe
moonquake
moonrise
moonrock
moonscape

moonset
moonshine (n., v.)
moonshiner/moonshining
moonshot
moonstone
moonstruck
moonwalk
mooring buoy (Nautical)
moot court
mopboard
moped (n.)
mopper-up
mopping-up (adj.)
mop-up (n.)
morning after
morning-after pill
morning coat
morning sickness
morning star
Morris chair
Morse code
mortal sin
mortarboard
mortise and tenon joint
mosh pit
mossback
moss green (n.)
moss-grown
most-favored-nation (adj.)
mothball(s)
moth-eaten
motherboard (Computers)
mother church
mother country
mother hen
Mother Hubbard
mother-in-law
motherland
mother lode
mother-naked
mother-of-pearl (n., adj.)
mother's helper

mothership
mother tongue
mother wit
mothproof
motion sickness
motion study
mot juste (F.): The appropriate word.
motley crew
motocross: A cross-country motorcycle race.
motorbike
motorboat
motorbus
motorcade
motorcar
motor home
motor inn
motor lodge
motorman
motor-minded
motor-mouth
motor pool
motor scooter
mountain bike
mountain dew
mountain range
mountaintop
mountebank
mourners' bench
mousehole
mousetrap
mouth organ
mouthpiece
mouth-to-mouth resuscitation
mouthwash
mouthwatering
movable feast
move-in (n.)
move-out (n.)
mover and shaker

moviegoer
moviegoing
moviemaker
movie theater
moving sidewalk
moving stairway
moving van
moving violation
mowing machine
Mr. Big
Mr. Charlie: A white man; white people.
Mr. Cool
Mr. Fix-It
Mr. Nice Guy
Mr. Right
Mrs. Grundy
Mr. Wrong
muckrake/muckraker
muck-up (n.)
muddlehead/ muddleheaded
muddle through
mudflow
mudguard
mudhole
mudpack
mudroom
mud slide
mudslinger/mudslinging
mud-wrestling
mug shot
muleheaded
mule skinner
mule train
mulligan stew
mulligatawny

NOTE: All words with the prefix *multi-* are written solid. Some examples:
    multicolor

multicultural
multidisciplinary
multifaceted
multifarious
multigenerational
multilayer
multilinear
multilingual
multimedia
multimillionaire
multiplicity
multiprogramming
multisyllable
multivitamin

multiple-choice
multiple-death (fire, etc.)
multiple listing
mumbletypeg
mumbo jumbo
murder one (two, etc.)
Murphy bed
Murphy's Law
musclebound
muscleman
museumgoer
museum piece
mushmouth
mushyheaded
musical chairs
musical comedy
music box
music hall
music of the spheres
music stand
mustache cup
mustard gas
must-see (n.)
Mutt and Jeff
mutual fund
muumuu: A Hawaiian dress.
muzzleloader

My Lai: Village in South
Vietnam.
mythmaker

N

NAFTA (North American
Free Trade Agreement)
nail-biting
nailbrush
nailclipper
nail file
nailhead
nail polish
namby-pamby
name brand [Hyphenate as
adj.]
name-caller/name-calling
name-drop (v.)
**name-dropper/
name-dropping**
name of the game
nameplate
namesake
nametag
nanometer
nanosecond
narrowcast (v., Radio and
TV)
narrowcasting
narrow gauge [Hyphenate
as adj.]
narrow-minded
narrow-mindedness
nation-state
nationwide
Native American (Indian)
native-born
native son
natural-born
natural childbirth

natural death
natural gas
natural history
natural selection
nature worship
navel orange
navy blue
navy yard
naysay (v.)
naysayer
neap tide
near beer
nearby
Near East
near miss
nearsighted
near-term
neat's-foot oil
neck and neck (adj., adv.)
neckband
neckline
necktie party: A hanging.
neckwear
needlecraft
needlepoint
needlework
ne'er-do-well (n., adj.)
negative feedback
negative income
neighborhood watch
neo-Nazi
ne plus ultra (L.)
nerve block
nerve cell
nerve center
nerve cord
nerve fiber
nerve gas
nerve-racking
nervous breakdown
nervous Nellie
nervous system

nest egg
net assets
netball (Tennis)
nethermost
netherworld
net profit
network (n., v.)
networking
nevermind (n.)
never-never land
nevertheless
new ball game
newborn (n., adj.)
newel post
newfangled
new-fashioned
newfound (adj.)
new look
new math
new-mint (v.)
news agency
newsagent
newsboy
newsbreak
newscast
news conference
newsdealer
newsdesk
news flash
newsletter
newsmagazine
newsmaker
newsman
newsmonger
newspaperman/
   newspaperwoman
newspeak
news peg
newsperson
newsprint
new-sprung (adj.)
newsreel

news release
newsroom
news service
newsstand
news story
newsvendor
newsweekly
newswire
newsworthy
newswriting
new town
new wave
next-door (adv., adj.)
next friend (Law)
next of kin
nice nelly [Hyphenate as
   adj.]
nice-nellyism
nickel-and-dime (adj., v.)
nickel plate (n.)
nickel-plate (v.)
nickname
Nielsen rating
night and day (n., adj.)
night-blind (adj.)
night blindness
nightcap
nightclothes
nightclub
night coach
night court
nightdress
night editor
nightfall
nightglow
nightgown
nighthawk
night latch
night letter
nightlife
night-light
nightlong

nightmare/nightmarish
night-night (interjec.)
night owl
night person
nightrider
night robe
night school
night shift
nightshirt
night soil
nightstand
night stick
night sweats
nighttime (n., adj.)
nightwalker
night watch
night watchman
nightwear
nighty-night
NIMBY: Not in my back yard.
nincompoop
nine days' wonder
ninepenny (nail)
ninepins
nineteenth hole
nine-to-five (adj.)
nine-to-fiver (n.)
ninety-day wonder
nip and tuck
Nissen hut
nitpick (v.)
nitpicker/nitpicking
nitric acid
nitric oxide
nitrogen mustard
nitroglycerin
nitrous acid
nitty-gritty
nitwit
no-account (adj., n.)
Nobel prize
no bill (Law)

noble gas
nobleman
noble metal
noble-minded
noblesse oblige (F.)
noblewoman
no-brainer
nodding acquaintance
no-fault (adj.)
no-frills (adj.)
no-go (adj.)
no-good (n., adj.)
no-goodnik
no-growth (adj., n.)
no-hit (adj.)
no-hitter
no-holds-barred (adj.)
nohow
noise factor
noisemaker
noise pollution
noiseproof
no-knock (adj.)
nolle prosequi (Law)
no-load (adj.)
nolo contendere (Law)
no-lose (adj.)
nol-pros (v.)
nol-prossed/nol-prossing
no man's land
nom de guerre (F.)
nom de plume (F.)

NOTE: With the exception of words containing a proper noun or adjective (e.g., *non-American, non-Biblical*) and a few combinations listed below, all words with the prefix *non-* are written solid. This includes *nondeductible, nonjuror, nonlawyer*, etc.

nonage: A period of youth.
no-name (adj.)
non-A, non-B hepatitis
nonce word
non compos mentis (Law)
nondairy
nondrinker
nonesuch (n., adj.)
nonetheless
nonfat
non grata (L.)
no-no (pl. **no-no's** or **no-nos**)
non-oil (an exception to the rule)
nonplus
nonproliferation
non sequitur (L.)
non-U
no one
noon hour
noontime
no-par
noplace
northbound
north by east/ north by west
northeast by east/ northeast by north
northeaster or **nor'easter**
northeastern
northernmost
north-northeast/ north-northeastward
north-northwest/ north-northwestward
North Pole
northwest by north/ northwest by west
northwester or **nor'wester**
northwestern
nose bag

noseband: Part of a bridle or harness.
nosebleed
nose candy (cocaine)
nose cone
nosecount
nosedive (n.)
nose-dive (v.)
nose drops
no-see-um: A biting midge.
nosegay
nose job
nose out (v.)
nosepiece
nosering
nosewheel (Aeronautics)
Nosey Parker (sometimes lowercase)
no-show (n., adj.)
no-strike (adj.)
no-strings (adj.)
no-sweat (adj.)
nota bene (L.): Note well.
notary public (pl. **notaries public**)
notchback (Automobile)
notebook
note broker
notecase
noteholder
note of hand: Promissory note.
notepad
notepaper
notereader
not-for-profit
NOT gate (Computers)
no-tillage (Farming)
no-trump (Bridge)
notwithstanding
nouveau riche (F.)
nouvelle cuisine (F.)

NOW account (Banking)
nowadays
nowheresville
no-win (adj.)
nowise (adv.)
nuclear family
nuclear fission
nudnik (Yid.): A pest; bore.
null and void
null-space (n., Mathematics)
number one: Oneself.
numero uno (It. or Sp.):
    Number one.
numskull, also numbskull
nuncupative will
nursemaid
nurse-practitioner
nurseryman
nursery school
nurse's aide
nursing home
nutbrown
nut case
nutcracker
nut house
nuts and bolts [Hyphenate
    as adj.]
nutshell

O

oak leaf cluster (Military)
oarlock
oarsman/oarsmanship
ob-gyn
obiter dictum (L.)
object ball (Pool or
    Billiards)
object lesson
objet d'art (F.)
obstacle course/

obstacle race
Occam's razor
oceanfront
oceangoing
oddball
Odd Fellow (lodge member)
odd job (v.)
odd lot
odd-lotter, also odd lotter
odd man out
odd or even
odds and ends
oddsmaker
odds-on (adj.)
Oedipus complex
off and on (adv.)
off-base (adj.)
offbeat (n., adj.)
off-board (adj., adv.)
off-brand (adj., n.)
off Broadway [Hyphenate
    as adj. or adv.]
off-budget (adj.)
off-camera (adj., adv.)
off-campus (adj., adv.)
offcast (n., adj.)
off-center (adj.)
off-color (adj.)
off-duty (adj.)
offhand (adj., adv.)
offhanded/offhandedly
off-hour (adv., adj.)
office boy
officeholder
officer of the day (Military)
office seeker
offish (adj.)
off-island/off-islander
off-key (adj.)
off-limits (adj.)
off-line (adj.)
off-load (v.)

off-mike (adj.)
off off Broadway
   [Hyphenate as adj. or adv.]
off-peak (adj.)
off-price (adj.)
offprint (n., v.)
off-putting (adj.)
off-ramp (n.)
off-road (adj., adv.)
offscouring (n.)
offscreen (adj., adv.)
off-season (n., adj., adv.)
offset/offsetting
offset lithography
offshoot (n.)
offshore (adv., adj.)
offshore dock
offshoreman
offside (adj., adv.)
off-site (adj., adv.)
off-speed (adj.)
offspring (n.)
offstage (adv.)
offtake (n.)
off-the-board (adj., adv.)
off-the-books (adj.)
off-the-cuff (adj.)
off-the-face (adj.)
off-the-job (adj.)
off-the-rack (adj.)
off-the-record (adj.): "Off
   the record, let's have an
   off-the-record talk."
off-the-shelf (adj.)
off-the-wall (adj.)
offtrack (adj.)
offtrack betting
off-white (adj.)
off year [Hyphenate as adj.]
oftentimes/ofttimes
ogee: A double curve.
ohmmeter

Ohm's law (Electricity)
oil burner
oil cake
oilcan
oilcloth
oil field
oil gland
oilman
oil paint/oil painting
oil pan
oilpaper
oil sand
oilseed
oil shale
oilskin
oil slick
oil spill
oilstone
oil tanker
oiltight
oil well
okey-doke/okey-dokey
old age
old boy (n.)
old-boy network
old country
oldfangled
old-fashioned (n., cocktail)
old-fashioned (adj.)
old fogy, also old fogey
old-fogyish (adj.)
old goat
old gold
old growth
Old Guard (often lowercase)
old hand
old hat
old lady
old-line (adj.)
old maid
old-maidish (adj.)
old man

old master
old mine cut (Jewelry)
old money
old school
old school tie
old shoe (n., adj.)
Old South
oldster
old style [Hyphenate as adj.]
Old Testament
old-time (adj.)
old-timer
Old West
old wives' tale
old-womanish (adj.)
Old World (Europe, Asia, and Africa)
old-world (adj.)
old-worldly (adj.)
olive branch
olive drab
olive green
olive oil
ombudsman
omnidirectional
on-again, off-again
on-air (adj.)
on and off
on and on
onboard (adj.)
on-camera (adj., adv.)
once and for all
once-over (n.): A quick look.
once-over-lightly (n.)
oncoming (adj.)
one-acter
one-armed bandit
one-bagger (Baseball)
one-base hit
one-dimensional
one-eighty (degrees)
one-eyed

onefold
one-handed
one-horse
one-legged
one-liner
one-man (adj.)
one-man show
one-nighter
one-night stand
one old cat: Form of baseball.
one-on-one
101 (as in Economics 101)
one-piece
one-point perspective
oneself or one's self
one-shot (n., adj.)
one-sided
one-size-fits-all (adj.)
one-star general
one-step (n., v.)
one-stop (adj.)
one-suiter (luggage)
onetime: Former.
one-time: Occurring only once.
one-to-one
one-track (mind, etc.)
one-two punch
one up (adj.)
one-up (v.)
one-upmanship
one-way (adj.)
one-woman (adj.)
one-worlder
ongoing
onionskin
on-line or online (adj., adv.; Computers, etc.)
onlooker/onlooking
on-mike (adj.)
on-peak (adj.)

on-ramp (n.)
on-record (adj.)
onrush/onrushing
on-screen (adj., adv.)
on-season (adj., adv.)
onset
onshore
onside (adj., adv.)
onside kick (Football)
on-site (adj.)
on-stage (adj., adv.)
on-stream (adj., adv.)
on-target (adj.)
on-the-cheap (adj.)
on-the-job (adj.)
on-the-record (adj.)
on-the-scene (adj.)
on-the-spot (adj.)
onto (prep., adj.) [Note: Do not use when *on* is an adverb. Correct: "We walked on to the school."]
op art
OPEC (Organization of Petroleum Exporting Countries)
op-ed or Op-Ed (n.)
op-ed page or Op-Ed page
open admissions
open air [Hyphenate as adj.]
open-and-shut (adj.)
open bar
open book [Hyphenate as adj.]
open call (Theater)
open chain (Chemistry)
open circuit
open city
open classroom
open convention (Politics)
open door [Hyphenate as adj.]

open-end (adj.)
open-ended (adj.)
open-end mortgage
open enrollment
open-eyed
open-faced
open field
openhanded (adj.)
openhandedly (adv.)
openhearted
openheartedly
open-hearth
open-heart surgery
open house
open housing
opening night
open letter
open-line (Radio or TV)
open loop (Computers)
open market
open marriage
open-minded
open-mindedly
open-mouthed
open policy
open season
open secret
open sesame
open-shelf (adj.)
open shop
open-sided
open sight (Firearms)
open space
open stack (Library Science)
open stock
open university
openwork
open-worked (adj.)
opera buffa (It.)
opera glasses
operagoer/operagoing

opera hat
opera house
operating room
operating system
opt out (v.)
order of the day
ordinary seaman
other-directed
other half
other man/other woman
other world
otherworldly
Ouija board

NOTE: All words with the prefix *out-* (with the exception of those that incorporate a proper noun, *out-Herod*, e.g.) are written solid. A few examples:
  outbuilding
  outdistance
  outdoorsman
  outmaneuver
  outnumber
  outscored
  outsource
  outsourcing
  outspeculated

out-and-out (adj.)
out-front (adj.)
out-of-body (adj.)
out-of-bounds (adv.)
out-of-court (adj.)
out-of-date (adj.)
out-of-doors (adj., n.)
out-of-pocket (adj.)
out-of-print (adj.)
out-of-sight (adj.)
out-of-state (adj.)
out-of-sync (adj.)

out-of-the-way (adj.)
out-of-town (adj.)
out-of-towner (n.)
outpatient
outward-bound (adj.)
Oval Office
ovenproof
ovenware

NOTE: All words listed in our dictionaries with the prefix *over-* are written solid. A few examples:
  overaggressive
  overambitious
  overcapacity
  overcompensate
  overpopulated
  overrepresented
  oversimplification
  overwrought

over and above
over and out
over and over
over easy (eggs, e.g.)
over with
owner-operator
oxblood
oxbow front (Furniture)
oxtail
oxygen mask
oyster white
ozone layer

P

pacemaker
pacesetter
package deal
package store

packboard
packhorse
packing case
packinghouse
packing plant
pack rat
paddleball
paddleboard
paddleboat
paddle wheel (Nautical)
paddy wagon
paddywhack (n., v.)
pageboy (hair style)
page boy (a boy)
page proof
page-turner
paid-in (adj.)
paid-in surplus
paid-up (adj.)
painkiller
painstaking
paintbox
paintbrush
paint pot
paint roller
pair bond (Animal Behavior)
pair-bond (v.)
pakapoo (Chinese lottery)
pale-dry (ginger ale, etc.)
paleface
palimony
pallbearer
pall-mall
palm leaf
palm off
Pan-American
pan-broil
pancake
Pandora's box
pandowdy
panelboard
pan-fry

pan gravy
panhandle
panic button
panic-stricken/panic-struck
pantaloon(s)
pant leg
pantsuit
panty girdle
pantyhose
panty raid
pantywaist
papal bull
paperback (n., adj.)
paperbacked
paperboard
paperbound
paperboy
paper chase
paper clip (n.)
paperclip (v.)
paper cutter
paper doll
papergirl
paperhanger/paperhanging
papermaker/papermaking
paper money
paper profit
paper-pusher
paper tape (Computers)
paper-thin
paper tiger
paper trail
paper-train (v.)
paperweight
paperwork
papier-mâché (F.; n., adj.)
Pap smear/Pap test

NOTE: Except for
para-aminobenzoic and
para-aminosalicylic, all words
in our dictionaries with the

prefix *para-* are written solid.
A few examples:
- paradoxical
- paraformaldehyde
- paragenesis
- parajournalism
- paralegal
- paramedical
- paranormal
- paraprofessional
- parapsychology
- parasympathetic

parcel post
parental leave
par excellence
par for the course
pari-mutuel machine
Paris green
parish house
parity check (Computers)
park-and-ride (n., adj.)
Parker House roll
parking lot
parking meter
Parkinson's disease
Parkinson's Law
parkland
parkway
parlor car
parlor game
parlormaid
parol evidence
parrot fever
particleboard
parti-colored
part of speech
part-score (Bridge)
part-time (adj., adv.)
part-timer
partway
party girl

partygoer
party line/party liner
party man
party politics
party pooper
party whip
par value
parvenu
pas de deux (F.)
passageway
passagework (Music)
passalong (n., adj.)
passbook
passe-partout (F.)
passerby (pl. passersby)
pass-fail (Education)
passing lane
passing note (Music)
passion play
passkey
pass muster (v.)
Passover
pass point (Surveying)
pass-through (n., adj.)
password
pasteboard
pastedown (n.)
paste-up (n.)
pastime
past master/past mistress
past participle (Grammar)
past perfect (Grammar)
past president
pastry blender
pastry tube
pastureland
pasty-faced
pat-a-cake
patchboard
patch cord
patch pocket
patch test

patch-up (n., adj.)
patchwork
pat-down (n.)
pâté de foie gras (F.)
patent leather
patent medicine
patent office
patent right
paterfamilias
paternity test
paternoster
pathfinder/pathfinding
pathway
patrol car
patrolman
patrol wagon
patron saint
pattern bargaining
pattern bombing
patternmaker/
   patternmaking
patty-cake: Pat-a-cake.
patty shell
pawnbroker/pawnbroking
pawnshop
pawn ticket
pay-as-you-go (n.)
payback
pay-cable
paycheck
payday
pay dirt
pay envelope
payload
payloader
paymaster
payoff (n.)
payola
payout (n.)
pay-per-view
pay phone
payroll

payroller
payroll tax
pay station
pay-TV
Peace Corps
peacekeeper/peacekeeping
peacemaker
peacenik
peace offering
peace officer
peace pipe
peace sign
peacetime
peaches-and-cream (adj.)
peachy-keen
pea jacket
peak flow meter
peanut butter
peanut gallery
pearl diver
Pearly Gates
peashooter
pea soup
peat bog
peat moss
pecking order
pedal boat
pedal point (Music)
pedal pushers
pedicab
peekaboo (n., adj.)
peel-and-stick (adj.)
peephole
Peeping Tom
peep show
peep sight (Firearms)
peer group
peer pressure
peewee
pegboard
Peg-Board™: A brand name
   for pegboard.

pegbox
peg leg
peg top (n., child's toy)
peg-top (adj.)
pell-mell (n., adj., adv.)
pellucid
penal code
penalty box (Ice Hockey)
penalty kick (Soccer)
penalty shot (Ice Hockey)
pencil box
pencil pusher
pencil stripe
penis envy
penknife
penlight
pen name
penny ante [Hyphenate as adj.]
penny arcade
penny dreadful
penny loafer
penny pincher
penny-pinching
penny stock (Stock Exchange)
pennyweight
penny-wise
pen pal
pen point
pension fund
pension plan
pentathlon (Sports)
penthouse
pent-up (adj.)
people mover
pepper-and-salt (adj., n.)
pepperbox
peppercorn
pepper mill
pepper pot
pepper shaker

pepper steak
pepper-upper
pep pill
pep rally
pep talk (n.)
peptalk (v.)
peptic ulcer
percent, also per cent
per diem
perfect pitch
performing arts
period piece
perk test
permafrost
permanent press
permanent wave
perma-press
pernickety or persnickety
perpetual motion
per se (L.)
persona grata (L.)
personal computer
personal effects
personal foul (Sports)
personal pronoun
personal property
persona non grata (L.)
person-to-person (adj.)
per stirpes (Law)
pesthole
pesthouse
petcock
Peter Principle
petit bourgeois (F.)
petit four (F.; pl. petits fours)
petit jury: Petty jury.
petit larceny
petit mal: Epilepsy.
petit point
pet name
pet-napping

pet peeve
petri dish
petrodollars
pet sitting
pettifog (v.)
pettifogger/pettifogging
petting zoo
petty cash
petty jury, also petit jury
petty larceny
petty officer
pewholder
phantom circuit
   (Electricity)
phantom limb pain
phantom stock
phasedown (n.)
phase-in (n.)
phaseout (n.)
Phi Beta Kappa
phone book
phone-in (n., adj.)
phonemail
phone sex
phony-baloney
photoautotroph
photocell (Electronics)
photocompose (v.)
photocomposer/
   photocomposition
photocopier
photocopy
photoelectricity
photoemission
photoengraving
photo finish
photofinishing
photojournalism
photomap (n., v.)
photo-mount (n.)
photomural
photo-offset (n., v.)

photo opportunity, also
   photo op
photoprint
photorealism
photoreception
photorecorder/
   photorecording
photoscan
photosensitivity
photo spread
Photostat™
photosystem
phototelegraphy
phototype
phototypesetting
phrase book
phrasemaker
phrasemonger
phys ed
physical therapy
physiotherapy
pia mater (Anatomy)
piano bar
pianoforte
piano tuner
piano wire
pickaback: Piggyback.
pick-and-shovel (adj.)
pickax (n., v.)
picket boat
picket fence
picket line
picklepuss
pick-me-up
pickoff (Baseball)
pickpocket
pickup (n.)
picosecond
picture layout
Picturephone™
picture tube
picture window

pidgin English
piebald
piece by piece (adv.)
pièce de résistance (F.)
piece dye (v.)
piece goods
piecemeal (adj., adv.)
piece of cake
piece of work
piece rate
piecewise (adv.,
   Mathematics)
piecework
pie chart
piecrust
pied-à-terre (F.)
Pied Piper (sometimes
   lowercase)
pie-eyed
pie-faced
pie in the sky
pier glass
pierhead
pier table
pigeon drop
pigeonhole
pigeon-livered
pigeon-toed
pigeonwing (Skating)
piggyback
piggyback car (Railroad)
piggy bank
pigheaded/pigheadedness
pig in a blanket (pl. pigs
   in blankets)
pig in a poke
pig iron
pig Latin
pig-out (n.)
pig out (v.)
pigpen
pigs' feet

pigskin
pigsty
pigtail
pile driver
pileup (n.)
pillbox
pillowcase
pillowslip
pillow talk
pill popper
pill pusher
pilot boat
pilot burner
pilot chart
pilot flag (Nautical)
pilothouse
pilot light
pilot signal
pilot whale
Piltdown man
piña cloth
piña colada
pinball machine
pince-nez (F.; eyeglasses)
pinch bottle
pinch hit (n.)
pinch-hit (v.)
pinch hitter
pinchpenny (n., adj.)
pinch runner
pin curl (n.)
pin-curl (v.)
pincushion
pine cone
pine tar
piney woods
pinfeather(s)
Ping-Pong™
ping-pong (v.): To move
   back and forth.
pinhead
pinhole

pink-collar (adj.)
pink elephants
pinkeye
pink lady (cocktail)
pink slip (n.)
pink-slip (v.)
pin money
pinpoint
pinprick
pins and needles
pinsetter
pin spot (n., Theater)
pin-spot (v.)
pinspotter
pinstripe/pinstriped
pint-size/pint-sized
pinup (n., adj.)
pinwheel
pipe bomb
pipe cleaner
pipe cutter
pipe dream (n.)
pipe-dream (v.)
pipe fitter/pipe fitting
pipe-layer
pipeline
pipeliner/pipelining
pipe of peace
pipe organ
pipe wrench
pipsqueak
pistol grip
pistol-whip (v.)
piston ring
piston rod
pitapat (n., adj., adv.)
pit boss
pitch-and-run shot (Golf)
pitch-and-toss
pitch-black
pitchblende
pitch-dark

pitched battle
pitchfork
pitch line
pitchman
pitchout (Baseball, Football)
pitch shot (Golf)
pitchstone
pitfall
pithead (Mining)
pitman (Mining)
pit stop
pitter-patter (n., v., adv.)
pivotman (Basketball)
pivot tooth
pixilated
placebo effect
place card
placeholder
place kick (n., Football)
place-kick (v.)
placename (n.)
place setting
plain clothes [Hyphenate as adj.]
plainclothesman
plain Jane [Hyphenate as adj.]
plain sailing
plainspoken
plain weave
plain-woven
plain-wrap (adj.)
planeload
plane table (n., Surveying)
plane-table (v.)
Planned Parenthood
planter's punch
plasterboard
plaster cast
plaster of Paris (last word sometimes lowercase)
plasterwork

plastic art
plastic bomb
plastic surgery
plasticware
plat du jour (F.)
plate block (Philately)
plate girder
plate glass
plateholder
platemaker
plate rail
plate tectonics
plateware
platform shoes
platinum blonde
playact (v.)
playacting (n.)
play-action pass (Football)
playback (n.)
playbill
playbook
playboy
playbroker
play-by-play (adj., n.)
playclothes
playdate
playday
play doctor (Theater)
playdown
playfellow
playgirl
playgoer
playground
playgroup
playhouse
playing card
playing field
playland
playmaker
playmate
play money
play-off (n.)

play on words
playpen
playreader
playroom
playscript
playstreet
playsuit
plaything
playtime
playwear
playwright
playwriting
plea-bargain (v.)
plea-bargaining (n.)
plein air (F.): The open air.
plein-air (adj.): Pertaining to
   a style of painting.
plenipotentiary
pleural cavity
plexiform
Plexiglas™
Plimsoll line
Plimsoll mark
plot line
plotting board
plotting sheet
plowback (n.)
plowboy/plowman
plowshare
plugboard
plugged-in (adj.)
plug-in (n., adj.)
plug-ugly
plumb bob
plumb line
plumb rule
plum pudding
plunk down
pluperfect (Grammar)
plus sight (Surveying)
plus sign
plywood

pocket battleship
pocketbook
pocket edition
pocket-handkerchief
pocketknife
pocket money
pocket piece
pocket-size
pocket veto (n.)
pocket-veto (v.)
pockmark/pockmarked
poetic justice
poetic license
poet laureate
point-blank (adj., adv.)
point count
point man
point of departure
point of honor
point of no return
point of order
point-of-purchase (adj.)
point-of-sale (n., adj.)
point of view
point shaving
point spread
point system
point-to-point (n.)
pointy-headed
poison gas
poison pen
poke check (Ice Hockey)
poker face [Hyphenate as adj.]
polar axis
polar bear
polar cap
polar front
polar lights
poleax
polecat
pole jump (n.)

pole-jump (v.)
pole vault (n.)
pole-vault (v.)
police dog
police force
police officer
police state
police station
policyholder
policymaker/policymaking
policyowner
politburo
political asylum
political science
polka dots
polka-dotted
polling booth
polling place
poll taker
poll tax
poll watcher
Pollyanna (n., adj.)
Pollyannaish (adj.)
pollywog
polo coat
polo shirt
poltergeist
pompom: An automatic gun; an ornamental ball.
pompom girl
pompon: Pompom; a flowering plant.
pond scum
pony express
ponytail
pony up (v.)
pooh-pooh
pool hall
poolroom
poolside
pool table
poop deck

pooper-scooper
poop sheet
poor box
poor boy: Hero sandwich.
poor farm
poorhouse
poor mouth (n.)
poor-mouth (v.)
poor-spirited
poor white trash
pop art
pop concert
popeyed
pop fly (Baseball)
popgun
pop-in (adj.)
popoff (n., adj.)
popout (n.)
popover: A muffin.
pop psych
poppycock
poppyseed
pop-top (adj., n.)
pop-up (adj., n.)
por favor (Sp.)
pork barrel
pork-barreler
pork belly
porkchop
porthole
portside (adv., adj.)
POSSLQ: Persons of opposite sex sharing living quarters.

NOTE: All words in our dictionaries with the prefix *post-* (except for those containing a capitalization) are written solid. A few examples follow, with phrases appearing in the regular alphabetical listing.
   postbellum

post-Darwinian
posthaste
postimpressionism
postmenstrual
postmeridian
postprandial

postage due stamp
postal card
postal order
postal service
postal union
postbox
postboy
postcard
poster child
post exchange
posthypnotic suggestion
postmark
post meridiem: P.M.
postmortem examination
postnasal drip
postnuptial agreement
post office
post-office box
postpaid
postpartum
post-season
potbelly
potboiler
pothead
pothole
pothook
pot liquor
potluck
pot of gold
potpie
potpourri (F.)
pot roast
potshot
potter's clay
potter's field

potter's wheel
potty-chair
poultryman
pound cake
pound-foolish (adj.)
pound sterling
poverty level
poverty-stricken
powder burn
powder horn
powder keg
powder puff [Hyphenate as
   adj.]
powder room
power base
powerboat/powerboater
powerbroker
power chain
power dive (n., Aeronautics)
power-dive (v.)
power drill
powerhouse
power mower
power of attorney
power pack
power plant
power play
power saw
power station
power takeoff
power tool
power train
powwow
practical nurse
practice-teach (v.)
prairie dog
praiseworthy
pratfall
prayer beads
prayer book
prayer meeting
prayer rug

prayer wheel

NOTE: All words with the
prefix *pre-* in our dictionaries, except those incorporating a capital letter
(*pre-Christian, pre-Gothic*,
e.g.), are written solid.

pre-British
Precambrian
pre-Christmas
prenuptial agreement
preowned
prep school
preschool/preschooler
presell
press agent
pressboard
press box
press bureau
press corps
press gallery
press gang (n.)
press-gang (v.)
press kit
press release
pressroom
pressrun
press secretary
press section
press time
pressure cabin
   (Aeronautics)
pressure-cook (v.)
pressure cooker
pressure point
pressure-treated
presswork
presumption of innocence
pretax (adj.)
preteen

preterm
preternatural
pretrial
pretty-pretty (adj.)
preventive medicine
price control
price-cut (v.)
price-cutter/price-cutting
price-earnings ratio
price fixing
price index
price list
price range
price support
price tag
price war
pride of place
prima ballerina
prima donna
prima facie
prima facie case
primal scream
primary care
primary cell
primary color
primary physician
primary school
prime interest rate
prime minister
prime mover
prime rate
prime ribs
prime time
primogenitor: Ancestor.
primogeniture: Firstborn; inheritance right belonging to eldest son.
primrose path
Prince Charming (often lowercase)
prince consort
printed matter

printer's error
printhead (Computers)
printing press
printmaker/printmaking
printout (n.)
printwheel
printworks
prison camp
prisoner of war
private eye
private label
private practice
private trust
privy council
privy seal
prix fixe (F.)
prizefight
prize ring
prizewinner/prizewinning
proabortion
proactive
pro-am (professional-amateur, Sports)
probable cause
pro-choice
profit and loss
profit sharing [Hyphenate as adj.]
profit taking (Stock Market)
pro forma (L.)
pro-life
promissory note
promptbook (Theater)
proof-of-purchase (n.)
proofread
proof sheet
proof spirit
propjet
propman
propyl group (Chemistry)
pro rata [Hyphenate as adj.]
prorate (v.)

pros and cons
prose poem
pro shop
prostyle (adj., Architecture)
pro tem/pro tempore (L.)
proud flesh
proudhearted
proving ground
prowl car
proximate cause
p's and q's
pseudo-events

NOTE: All other words with the prefix *pseudo-* (except those incorporating a capital letter, *pseudo-French,* e.g.) are written solid.

psychic bid (Bridge)
psych-out (n.): An act or instance of psyching someone out.
psych up (v.)
pub crawl (n.)
pub-crawl (v.)
public-access TV
public charge
public domain
Public Enemy Number One
public eye
public health
public school
public-spirited
puck-carrier (Ice Hockey)
puddle-jumper
puff paste
puff piece
pug nose
pug-nosed
Pulitzer Prize
pullback (n.)

pulldown (n., Movies)
pull-down (adj.)
pull hitter (Baseball)
pull-off (n.)
pull-on (n., adj.)
pullout (n., adj.)
pullover (n., adj.)
pull-tab
pull-up (n.)
pulpboard
pulpwood
pulsebeat
pulse-code modulation
pulse-jet engine
pulse rate
pump-action (Firearms)
pump box
pumpernickel
pump gun
pump house
pumpkinseed
pump priming
pump room
Punch-and-Judy show
punchball
punchboard
punch bowl
punch card
punch-drunk
punching bag
punch line
punch list
punch-out (n.)
punch press
punch-up (n., Brit.)
punch up (v.)
punk rock
punt formation
puppy dog
puppy love
pup tent
pureblood (n., adj.)

pureblooded or
  pure-blooded (adj.)
purebred (adj., n.)
purehearted
pure line (Genetics)
pure reason (Kantianism)
Purple Heart
purse-proud
purse seine/purse seiner
purse strings
purse-string suture
pushback (n.)
pushball
push broom
push button [Hyphenate as
  adj.]
pushcart
pushdown (Computers)
push-in (adj.)
pushout (n.)
pushover (n.)
pushpin
push-pull (n., adj.)
push shot (Basketball)
push-up (n., adj.)
pussycat
pussyfoot (v., n.)
pussy willow
put-and-take (n.)
put-down
putdownable: Said of an
  unexciting book, e.g.
put-off (n.)
put-on (n., adj.)
put-out (n., Baseball)
put-put (n., v.)
putting green
put-up (adj.)
put-upon (adj.)
puzzle box
puzzleheaded: Confused.
pyramid bet

Pyrrhic victory

Q

Q and A, also Q&A
Q-ratio
Q-Tip™
quadrate (adj., n., v.)
quadricentennial
quad right (Computers)
quadrilateral
quadrilingual
quadriplegic
quadruplicate
quality control
quality-of-life (adj.)
quantum jump/
  quantum leap
quarterback
quarterfinal (adj., n.; Sports)
quarterfinalist
quarter horse
quarter-hour
quartermaster
quartersawed/quartersawn
quarter tone (Music)
quartz crystal
quartz glass
quartz lamp

NOTE: Nearly all words with
the prefix *quasi-* retain the
hyphen following the prefix.
(Exceptions: *quasi contract,
quasiparticle.*) Some examples:
  quasi-judicial
  quasi-legal
  quasi-legislative
  quasi-official
  quasi-qualified

quasi-serious
quasi-subconscious

queen bee
Queen's English
queenship
queen-size
question mark
question of fact
question of law
quiche Lorraine
quick-and-dirty (adj.)
quick assets
quick bread
quick-change artist
quick draw
quick fix
quick-freeze (v.)
quick kick (Football)
quicklime
quicksand
quick-setting
quicksilver
quickstep
quick study
quick-tempered
quick time (n.)
quickwater
quick-witted
quid pro quo (L.)
quilting bee
quintessence
quintessential
quitclaim (n., v.)
quitclaim deed
qui vive (F.): Who goes there? To be on the qui vive is to be alert.
quiz kid
quizmaster
quiz show
quod erat demonstrandum

(L.): Which was to be demonstrated.
quondam: Former.
quota system
quoteworthy
quo warranto (L.)

R

rabbet joint (Carpentry)
rabbit ears
rabbit fever
rabbit punch
rabbit's foot
rabble-rouser/
    rabble-rousing
raceabout: A small yacht.
racecourse
racehorse
race riot
racetrack
race-walk (v.)
race walking
raceway
racing car
racing form
rack and pinion
    [Hyphenate as adj.]
rack and ruin: Wrack and ruin.
rack-rent (n.)
rack up
radiant heat
radical left/radical right
radioactive fallout
radioactive waste
radio car
radiocarbon dating
ragamuffin
ragbag
ragged edge

raggle-taggle
ragpicker
ragtag and bobtail
ragtime
rah-rah
railbird
railcar
rail fence
railhead
rail-splitter
rainband
rain check
rain cloud
rain dance
rain date
rain forest
rain gauge
rainmaker/rainmaking
rainout
rainproof
rain shower
rainspout
rainsquall
rainstorm
rainwash
rainwater
rainwear
rainy day
raison d'être (F.): Reason for living.
rakehell (n., adj.)
rake-off (n.)
rallymaster
ramshackle
ranch house
ranchman
random access (n., Computers)
random-access (adj.)
random sampling
R and R, also R&R: Rest and relaxation.

range finder
rangeland
rank and file [Hyphenate as adj.]
rank-and-filer: A member of the rank and file.
rap group
rapid eye movement
rapid fire [Hyphenate as adj.]
rapid transit
rap music
rap session
rap sheet: A police arrest record.
rara avis (L.): A rarity.
rare book
rare earth
rat-a-tat or rat-a-tat-tat
ratatouille
ratbite fever
ratcatcher
rat cheese
ratchet wheel
rate base
rate card
rated load
ratemeter
ratepayer
rat fink
rathole
rathskeller
ratline (Nautical)
rat pack
rat race
rattail
rattail comb
rat-tail file
rattlebrain/rattlebrained
rattletrap
rattrap
rattrap cheese: Cheddar.

rawboned
raw deal
raw fibers
rawhide
raw material
raw score
raw silk
razzle-dazzle
razzmatazz

NOTE: Most words with the prefix *re-* are written solid. (There are a few exceptions, such as *re-create, re-cover, re-up*.) The *re-* prefix words are intermingled below.

readback
read-only (Computers)
read-only memory
readout (n., Computers)
readthrough
read/write head (Computers)
ready-made (adj., n.)
ready-mix (n., adj.)
ready money
ready-to-wear
ready-witted
Reaganomics
reagent
real estate [Hyphenate as adj.]
realign
reality-based (adj.)
reality check
real-life (adj.)
real number (Mathematics)
realpolitik
real property
realtime (Court Reporting)
real time (Computers)

real-time (adj.)
reapportion
reappraise
rear admiral
rear echelon
rear end [Hyphenate as adj. or v.]
rear-ender
rear guard
rearmost
rear view mirror
rearward
reasonable doubt
reclaim: To bring wasteland, etc., into condition for cultivation.
re-claim: To claim again.
recollect: To recall to mind.
re-collect: To collect again.
recombine
recordkeeping
recover: To get back or regain something.
re-cover: To cover again.
recreate: To take recreation.
re-create: To create again.
recross examination
red alert
red-bait (v.)
red-baiting (n.)
red blood cell
red-blooded
red carpet
redcoat: British soldier.
red corpuscle
red count
red devil
red dog: A gambling game.
red-dog (v., Football)
red-eye: Cheap, strong whiskey.
red-eyed

red-faced
red flag
red-green blindness
red-handed
redhead
redheaded
red herring
red-hot (n., adj.)
redingote
red ink
redirect examination
red lead: A poisonous powder.
red-letter (adj.)
red light (n.)
red-light (v., adj.)
red-light district
red line (Ice Hockey)
redline (n.): Recommended safety limit.
redline (v.): To treat by redlining a district.
redlining: A discriminatory practice of some banks, insurance companies, etc.
red meat
redneck (n., adj.)
redo
redoubt (n., Fortification)
redout: A condition experienced by pilots.
red-pencil (v.)
red pepper
redshirt (n., v.; varsity athletics)
redskin
red tag (n.)
red-tag (adj., v.)
red tape
red tide
redux (adj.)
redwood

reecho
reed organ
reeducate
reel-to-reel (adj.)
reemerge
reengage
reengineering: Downsizing.
reentry vehicle
reexamine
reform (n., v.): To change to a better state.
re-form (v.): To form again.
refried beans
rehab (n., adj.)
rehabbed/rehabbing
rehash
rehearing (Law)
release: To free from confinement.
re-lease: To lease again.
relief map
relief pitcher
relief valve
remark: To say casually.
re-mark: To mark again.
remote control [Hyphenate as adj.]
rent-a-car
rent control
rent-free (adj., adv.)
repetitive strain injury
report card
reprove: To criticize or correct.
re-prove: To prove again.
requiescat in pace (L.)
res adjudicata: Lawyers say it, but *res judicata* is preferred.
research: To investigate.
re-search: To search again.
res gestae (Law)

resign: To give up an office, etc.

re-sign: To sign again.

res judicata (L.): A thing adjudicated.

resort: To have recourse for help, etc.

re-sort: To sort again.

resound: To echo or ring with sound.

re-sound: To sound again.

rest cure

rest home

rest room

rest stop

retread: To put a new tread on.

re-tread: To tread (walk) again.

retreat: To withdraw.

re-treat: To treat again.

re-up: To reenlist.

reverse angle shot (Movies)

reverse-engineer (v.): To study or analyze a device to learn details of design, etc.

reverse English (Billiards)

rewriteman

Reye's syndrome

rheumatic fever

Rh factor

rhyme or reason

rhythm and blues

rhythm band

rhythm method

rib cage

rib eye (beefsteak)

rib-knit (adj.)

rib roast

rib-tickling

rice paper

ridesharing (adj.)

riffraff

rifleman

rifle range

rigamarole

rightabout (n., adv.)

right about face (Military)

right angle

right-angled

right brain

right face (Military)

right field (Baseball)

right hand (n.)

right-hand (adj.)

right-handed/right-hander

right-hand man

right-minded

right-of-center (adj.)

right of search

right of way

right on (interjec.)

right stuff

right thinking

right-to-die (adj.)

right-to-know (adj.)

right-to-life (adj.)

right-to-work (adj.)

right-to-work law

right wing

right-winger

rigor mortis

ring-around-the-rosy

ring binder

ring finger

ringleader

ringmaster

ringside/ringsider

rinky-dink

riot act

riot gun

riparian right (Law)

rip cord

ripoff (n.)

ripple effect
riprap (n., v.)
rip-roaring
ripsaw
ripsnorter
riptide
risk-benefit (adj.)
risk capital
risktaker
rite of passage
riverbank
river basin
riverbed
riverboat
riverfront
riverside
roach clip: Used by marijuana smokers.
roadability
roadbed
roadblock (n., v.)
road gang
road hog
roadhouse
road kill
road map
road show [Hyphenate as adj.]
roadside
road test (n.)
road-test (v.)
roadway
roadwork
roadworthy
roasting ear
robber baron
robot bomb
rockabilly
rock-and-roll: Rock-'n'-roll.
rock and rye
rock bottom [Hyphenate as adj.]

rockbound
rocket bomb
rocket gun
rocket launcher
rocket-propelled
rocket scientist
rocket ship
rockfall
rock garden
rock hound
rocking chair
rocking horse
rock-'n'-roll/rock-'n'-roller
rock-ribbed
rodman
rogues' gallery
role model
role-play (v.)
role-playing
roll-around (adj.)
rollaway (adj., n.)
rollback (n.)
roll call
roller bearing
Rollerblades™
roller coaster (n.)
roller-coaster (v.)
roller mill
roller skate (n.)
roller-skate (v.)
roller towel
rolling mill
rolling pin
rolling stock
roll-off (n.)
roll-on (adj., n.)
rollout (n.)
rollover (n.)
roll top
roll-top desk
roll-up (n.)
rollway

roly-poly
romper room
roof-deck
roof garden
roofline
rooftop
rooftree
room and board
room clerk
rooming house
roommate
room mother
room service
root beer
root canal
root cellar
rootstock
ropedancer
ropemaking
ropewalker
ropeway
rose-colored glasses
rose water [Hyphenate as
  adj.]
Rosh Hashanah: Jewish high
  holy day.
rotary dial
rotary plow
rotator cuff
rototill
rototiller
rottenstone
rough-and-ready (adj.)
rough-and-tumble (n., adj.)
roughcast (n., v.)
rough cut (Movies)
rough-cut (adj.)
rough-dry (v., adj.)
rough-hewn (adj.)
roughhouse
roughing-in (Building
  Trades)

roughneck (n., adj.)
roughrider
rough-sawn
roughshod
rough-spoken
rough stuff
rough-voiced
roundabout (n., adj.)
roundheaded
roundhouse
round-off (adj., n.;
  Mathematics)
round robin
round-shouldered
roundsman
round steak
round table
round-the-clock
round trip (n.)
round-trip (adj.)
roundup
roustabout
routeman
rowboat
row house
royal flush (Poker)
R-rated
rubber band
rubber-base paint
rubber bridge
rubber cement
rubber check
rubber-chicken circuit
rubber-faced
rubberneck (v., n.)
rubber stamp (n.)
rubber-stamp (v.)
rubber tree
rubbing alcohol
rubdown
Rube Goldberg
ruboff (n.)

rubout (n.)
rucksack
rudderhead/rudderpost
(Nautical)
rule of the road
rule of thumb
rumble seat
rumdum: Stupid or ignorant
person; drunkard.
rummage sale
rumormonger
rumpus room
rumrunner
runabout (n.)
runaround (n.)
runaway (n., adj.)
runback (Football, Tennis)
rundown (n.)
run-down (adj.)
run-in (n.)
runner-up
running back (Football)
running board
running knot
running mate
running start
running stitch
running time
runoff
run-of-the-mill
run-of-the-mine
run-on (n., adj.)
run-on sentence
runout (n.)
runover (n., Printing)
run-over (adj.)
runproof
run-through (n., adj.)
runup (n.)
runway
rural delivery (formerly
rural free delivery)

rural route
rush hour
rust-colored
rustproof/rustproofing
rye bread
rye whiskey

S

saber rattling
saber-toothed
sackcloth
sack coat/sack dress
sack race
sack suit
sack time
sacred cow
saddlebag
saddle blanket
saddle block anesthesia
saddlecloth
saddle horn
saddle horse
saddle seat
saddle soap
saddle sore (n.)
saddlesore (adj.)
saddle stitch
saddletree
sad-faced
sad sack
safari suit
safe-conduct (n.)
safecracker/safecracking
safe-deposit
safe-deposit box
safeguard
safe harbor
safe house
safekeeping
safe period

safe sex
safety belt
safety-deposit box: Safe-deposit box.
safety glass
safety lamp (Mining)
safety lock
safety net
safety pin (n.)
safety-pin (v.)
safety razor
safety valve
sagebrush
sailboard/sailboarding
sailcloth
sailplane
sail-over (Yachting)
salad bar
salad days
salad oil
sales check
salesclerk
saleslady/salesman
salesperson
sales promotion
sales slip
sales tax
Sallie Mae: Student Loan Marketing Association.
sal soda
salt-and-pepper (adj.)
saltbox
saltcellar
salt flat
salt lake
salt lick
salt marsh
saltpeter
salt pork
salt shaker
saltwater (adj.)
saltworks

salty dog
sam hill: What in sam hill is going on?
sampan
sanctum sanctorum (L.)
sandbag
sandbank
sand bar
sandblast (n., v.)
sandbox
sand-cast (v.)
sand casting
sand dollar
sandhog
sand jack
sandlot
S and M or S&M: Sadism and masochism; sadist and masochist.
sandman
sandpile
sandpiper
sandpit
sand-sprayed (adj., Building Trades)
sandstone
sandstorm
sand trap (Golf)
sandwich board
sandwich man
sang-froid (F.): Coolness of mind.
sanitary landfill
sanitary napkin
sanitary ware
sans serif (Printing)
Santa Ana: Wind.
saturated fat
saturation point
Saturday night special: Cheap handgun.
saucepan

saucer dome (Architecture)
save-all (n.)
saving grace
savings account
savings and loan bank
savior-faire (F.): Knowledge of what to do in any situation.
sawbones
sawbuck
sawed-off (adj.)
sawhorse
sawmill
sawtoothed
say-so
scalawag
scaledown (n.)
scaleup (n.)
scandalmonger/
    scandalmongering
scandal sheet
scapegoat
scarecrow
scaredy-cat
scaremonger
scar-faced
scarf joint
scarlet fever
scar tissue
scatterbrain
scatter rug
scattershot (adj.)
scavenger hunt
sceneshifter
scene-stealer
schlemiel (Yid.): A bungler.
schlockmeister
schmierkase: Cottage cheese.
Scholastic Aptitude Test
school age [Hyphenate as adj.]

schoolbag
school board
schoolbook
schoolboy/schoolgirl
school bus
schoolchild
school day
schoolhouse
schoolmarm
schoolmaster
schoolmate
schoolroom
schoolteacher/
    schoolteaching
schoolteacherish
schooltime
schoolwork
schoolyard
school year
science fiction
sci-fi (adj.)
scissors hold
scissors kick (Swimming)
sci-tech
scofflaw
scorched-earth policy
scoreboard
scorecard
scorekeeper
Scotchgard™
scot-free (adv., adj.)
Scotland Yard
scout car
scoutmaster
scrapbook
scrap heap
scratch line
scratch pad
scratchproof
scratch sheet
screaming-meemies
screen grid

screenplay
screen saver
screen test (n.)
screen-test (v.)
screenwriter
screwball
screw cap
screwdriver
screw thread
screw-top (adj.)
screw-up (n.)
scrimmage line
scrimshaw
script reader
scriptwriter
scroll saw
scrollwork
scrub brush
scrubdown (n.)
scrubland
scrub suit
scrub-up (n.)
scrubwoman
scuba-dive (v.)
scuba diver/scuba diving
scumbag
scuttlebutt
scutwork
sea bag
seabed
seaboard (n., adj.)
seaborne
sea breeze
sea change: Transformation.
sea chest
seacoast
seacock
sea dog: A sailor.
seafarer/seafaring
seafloor
sea foam
seafood

seagoing
sea gull
sea horse
seajack/seajacker
sea-lane
sea-launched ballistic
    missile
sealed book
sea legs
sea level
sealift
seal ring
sealskin
seaplane
seaport
sea power
seaquake
searchlight
search party
search warrant
seascape
sea serpent
seashell
seashore
seaside
seat belt
seatmate
seat-of-the-pants (adj.)
seatrain
sea wall
seaward
seawater
seaway
seaworthy
second base/
    second baseman
second best (n.)
second-best (adj.)
second-class (adj.)
second-degree burn
second-degree murder
second fiddle

second-generation (adj.)
second-guess (v.)
second hand (n.): On a
   timepiece.
second hand (n.): An inter-
   mediate person or means
   (We learned it at second
   hand).
secondhand (adj.): Not
   directly known or experienced; not new.
secondhand smoke
second-rate (adj.)
second sex
second sight
second-story (adj.)
second-story man
second string [Hyphenate
   as adj.]
second thought
second wind
secret agent
secretary-general
secret police
secret service
security blanket
security risk
seedbed
seedcake
seed corn
seed money
seed pearl
seedpod
Seeing Eye dog
seersucker
seesaw
see-through (adj., n.)
seismic sea wave
selectman

NOTE: Except for *selfish* and
selfless (and their deriva-

tives), *selfsame*, and a few
words seldom heard
(*selfdom, selfhood, selfness,*
and *selfward*), all words with
the prefix *self-* are hyphenated.

seller's market
selling point
sell-off (Stock Exchange)
sellout (n.)
semester hour

NOTE: Words with the prefix
semi- followed by the letter *i*
(*semi-illiterate, semi-indirect,*
e.g.) are hyphenated. All oth-
ers in our dictionaries are
written solid.

semiconductor
semiconscious
semidarkness
semigloss
semifinalist
semi-independent
semimonthly/
   semiweekly/semiyearly

seminal fluid
semper fidelis (L.): Motto of
   the U.S. Marine Corps.
send-off (n.)
send-up (n.)
septic tank
sequential-access (adj.,
   Computers)
sergeant at arms
series-wound (adj.,
   Electricity)
serious-minded
serviceman
service station

servocontrol (n., v.)
servomechanism
sesquicentennial
sesquipedalian
set-aside (n., adj.)
setback (n.)
set-in (adj.)
setoff (n.)
setout (n.)
set piece (Fireworks, etc.)
setpoint: Desired value in a closed-loop feedback system.
set point (Tennis)
set shot (Basketball)
setting-up exercise
settling tank
set-to (n.; pl. set-tos)
set-top (adj.)
set-top boxes
setup (n.)
seven-card stud
seven-eleven
seven-league boots
seventh-inning stretch
seven up (card game)
Seven-Up or 7-Up™
Seven Wonders of the World
seven-year itch
seven-year locust
sewing circle
sex appeal
sex change
sexed-up (adj.)
sex hormone
sex kitten
sex-linkage (Genetics)
sex-linked
sex object
sex play
sexpot

sex shop
sex symbol
sexually transmitted disease
shabby-genteel
shacking up
shackup (n.)
shade-grown
shadow band
shadow box (n.)
shadow-box (v.)
shadowland
shaft alley (Nautical)
shagbark
shaggy-dog story
shakedown (n.)
shake down (v.)
shakeout (n.)
shake-up (n.)
shamefaced
Shangri-la
shankpiece
shanks' mare
shantytown
shape-up (n.)
shape up (v., or ship out)
sharecrop/sharecropper
shareholder
shark repellent (n.)
sharkskin
sharp-cut (adj.)
sharp-eared (adj.)
sharp-edged (adj.)
sharp-eyed (adj.)
sharp-nosed (adj.)
sharpshooter
sharp-sighted (adj.)
sharp-tongued (adj.)
sharp-witted (adj.)
shavetail
shaving brush/ shaving cream

shear pins
sheath knife
she-devil
sheep's eyes
sheepshank
sheet glass
sheet metal
Sheetrock™
shelf life
shell game
shellproof
shell shock
shell-shocked (adj.)
shepherd's pie
she-wolf
shilly-shally (adj., adv., v., n.)
shinbone
shindig
shin guard
ship biscuit
shipboard
shipbuilder
shipfitter
shipmaster
shipmate
ship of state
shipowner
ship-rigged
shipshape
shipside
ship's store
ship-to-shore (adj., adv.)
shipwreck
shipwright
shipyard
shirtdress
shirt front
shirtmaker
shirtsleeve
shirttail
shirtwaist
shish ke-bab, also

shish ke-bob
shock absorber
shocking pink
shockproof
shock-resistant
shock-test (v.)
shock therapy
shock troops
shock wave
shoemaker
shoofly pie
shoo-in (n.)
shoot-'em-up
shooting gallery
shooting match
shoot-off (n.)
shootout (n.)
shoot-the-chutes
shoot-up (n.)
shopcraft
shopgirl
shopkeeper
shoplift (v.)
shoplifter
shopping bag
shopping-bag lady
shopping list
shopping mall/
   shopping plaza
shoptalk
shopwindow
shopworn
shorebird
shore dinner
shorefront
shore leave
shoreline
shore patrol
shoreside
shoreward
short ballot
shortbread

shortcake
shortchange (v.)
shortchanger (n.)
short circuit (n.)
short-circuit (v.)
shortcoming
shortcut
short-day (adj.)
shortfall
short field (Baseball)
short fuse
shorthaired
shorthanded
short-haul (adj.)
shorthorn
short line (Transportation)
short list (n.)
shortlist (v.)
short-lived (adj.)
short order [Hyphenate as adj.]
short-range (adj.)
short rate (Insurance)
short ribs
short-run (adj.)
short sale
short seller
short short story
short shrift
shortsighted
shortsleeved
short-spoken (adj.)
shortstop
short-tempered
short-term
short-term memory
short-timer
short ton
short-waisted
shortwave (adj., n., v.)
short weight (n.)
short-weight (v.)

short-winded
shot effect (Electronics)
shot glass
shotgun wedding
shot hole
shot put (n., Sports)
shot-putter/shot-putting
shoulder bag
shoulder blade
shoulder-length
shoulder patch
shoulder strap
shouting match
show and tell [Hyphenate as adj.]
show bill
show biz
showboat
show business
showcase (n., v., adj.)
show cause order (Law)
showdown (n.)
shower bath
showerhead
showerproof
shower stall
showman/showmanship
show-me (adj.)
show-off
showpiece
showplace
showroom
show-stopper
showtime
show trial
show window
shuffleboard
shunpike (n., v.)
shutdown
shut-eye
shut-in
shutoff

shutout
shutterbug
shuttlecock
shuttle diplomacy
sick bay
sickbed
sick call
sick day
sick leave
sickle cell anemia
sickout
sick pay
sickroom
side arm: A weapon.
sidearm (adv., adj.)
side band (Radio)
sidebar (n., adj.)
side bet
sideboard
sideburns
side by side (adv.)
sidecar
side dish
side effect
side-glance
sidekick
sidelight
sideline (n., v.)
sideliner
sidelong glance
side-on (adj., adv.)
sidepiece
sidereal time (Astronomy)
sidesaddle
sideshow
sideslip (v., n.)
sidespin
sidesplitter/sidesplitting
side step (n.)
sidestep (v.)
side street
sidestroke (Swimming)

sideswipe
sidetrack (v., n.)
side trip
sidewalk artist
sidewalk sale
sidewall
sideward(s)
sideways
sidewheel (Nautical)
side-wheeler
side-whiskers
sidewind (v.)
sidewinder
sidewise
siege mentality
sight draft
sight gag
sightline
sight-read (v.)
sight reader
sight rhyme
sightsee
sightseeing
sight unseen
signal board
signboard
signet ring
significant other
sign-in (n.)
sign language
sign-off (n.)
sign of the cross
sign-on (n.)
signpost
sign-up (n.)
silent alarm
silent auction
silent partner
silica gel
silk screen or silkscreen
   (n.)
silk-screen or silkscreen (v.)

silk stocking [Hyphenate as adj.]
silkworm
sillcock
Silly Putty™
silver cord
silver fox
silver plate (n.)
silver-plate (v.)
silver-plated (adj.)
silver screen
silversmith
silver spoon
silver standard
silver-tongued
silverware
silver wedding
s'il vous plaît (F.)
Simon Legree
simon-pure
simpatico
simple-hearted
simpleminded
Simple Simon
sine die (L.)
sine qua non (L.): Essential thing.
singalong
single-acting/single-action (Firearms)
single-barrel (Firearms)
single-blind (adj., experiment)
single-breasted
single-digit
single-ended
single entry (Bookkeeping)
single-family
single file
single-hand (v., Nautical)
single-handed/ single-handedly

single-hearted/ single-heartedness
single-knit (n.)
single-minded
single-phase (adj.)
singles bar
single-sex (adj.)
single-space (v.)
single-spaced
single tax
single-track (adj.)
single-valued
Sing Sing
singsong
sinkhole
sinking fund
sinking spell
Sinn Fein (Irish politics)
sin tax
siren song
sister-in-law
sitcom
sit-down (adj., n.)
sit-down strike
sit-in (n.)
sitting duck
sitting room
sit-up (n.)
sitz bath
sitzkrieg (G.): Nonaggressive warfare.
sitzmark (Skiing)
sixfold
six-footer
six-pack
sixpenny nail
six-shooter
sixth sense
size-up (n.)
skateboard/skateboarding
skedaddle
skeet shooting

skeleton key
sketchbook
skewback (Architecture)
skewbald (adj., n.)
skew curve
skew lines
ski boot
skid mark
skidproof
skid row
ski jump
ski lift
ski mask
skim milk
skimobile
skin and bones
skin-deep
skin-dive (v.)
skin diving
skinflint
skinful
skin game
skin graft
skinhead
skinny-dip (v.)
skin-pop: To inject drugs
   subcutaneously.
skin test
skintight
skip-bomb (v.)
skip bombing
skipjack: A small sailboat.
ski-plane
ski pole
skirt chaser
ski run
ski suit
ski tow
skivvy shirt
skiwear
skulduggery
skull and crossbones

skullcap
skull session
sky blue
skyborne
skycap
skydive (v.)
skydiving
sky-high
skyhook
skyjack (v.)
skyjacking
skylark
skylight
skylighted or skylit (adj.)
skyline
skylounge
sky marshal
sky pilot
skyrocket
skyscape
skyscraper
skytrooper
skywalk
skyway
skywrite (v.)
skywriting
slab-sided
slackjawed
slack suit
slack water
slam-bang (adv., adj., v.)
slam dunk (n., Basketball)
slam-dunk (v.)
slant-eyed
slantways/slantwise
slapdash
slaphappy
slapjack: A pancake; a card
   game.
slap shot (Ice Hockey)
slapstick (n., adj.)
slash-and-burn (adj.)

slash pocket
slate-blue
slaughterhouse
slave driver
slaveholder
slave labor
slave state
sleazebag
sledgehammer
sleep apnea
sleep-away (adj., adv.)
sleep-in (adj., n.)
sleeping bag
sleeping car
sleeping pill
sleep-out (adj., n.)
sleepover (n.)
sleepwalk (v., n.)
sleepwalking
sleepwear
sleepyhead
sleigh bells
sleight of hand
sleuthhound
slice-of-life (adj.)
slide-action (adj., Firearms)
slide fastener
slide knot
slide rule
slide valve
sliding scale
slimline (adj.)
slimnastics
slingshot
slipcover
slip form (n.)
slipform (v.)
slipknot
slip noose
slip-on (adj., n.)
slipover (n., adj.)
slipped disk

slipshod
slipslop: Meaningless talk or writing.
slipstitch (n., v.; Sewing)
slipstream (n., v.)
slip-up (n.)
slipway (Nautical)
sloe-eyed
sloe gin
slop-over (n.)
sloppy joe
slot machine
slow burn
slowdown (n.)
slow-footed
slow-mo
slow motion [Hyphenate as adj.]
slow-moving
slow-pitch (n., Softball)
slowpoke
slow-up (n.)
slow-wave sleep
slow-witted
slugabed
slugfest
sluiceway
slumberland
slumber party
slumdweller
slumgullion
slumlord
slush fund
slush pile (Publishing)
slyboots
smack-dab
smackeroo
small arms (Firearms)
small beer
small-bore (Firearms)
small change
small-claims court

small craft advisory
small fry
small game
small hours
small-minded
small potatoes
small print
small-scale (adj.)
small screen
small stuff
small talk
small time [Hyphenate as adj.]
small-town (adj.)
smart aleck
smart-alecky
smart-ass
smart bomb
smart money
smart set
smarty-pants
smash hit
smashup
smear campaign
smear-sheet
smelling salts
smithereens
smoke detector
smoke-dry (v.)
smoke-eater
smoke-filled room
smokehouse
smoke pot
smokeproof
smoke screen
smoke shop
smokestack
smoking gun
smoking jacket
smoothbore (adj., n.; Firearms)
smooth-faced

smooth-shaven
smooth-spoken
smooth-talk (v.)
smooth-tongued
smudge pot
snack bar
snaggletooth
snail mail (facetious)
snail-paced
snail's pace
snakebite
snake charmer
snake dance (n.)
snake-dance (v.)
snake doctor
snake eyes (Craps)
snake-hipped
snake in the grass
snake oil
snake pit
snakeskin
snapback (Football)
snap course
snap fastener
snap-in (adj.)
snap link
snap-off (adj.)
snap-on (adj.)
snap ring (Machinery)
snap roll (n., Aeronautics)
snap-roll (v.)
snapshoot (v.)
snapshooter
snapshot
snare drum
snatch block (Nautical)
sneak preview
sneak thief
sneaky pete
sniperscope: A snooper-scope.
Sno-Cat™

snollygoster: A clever,
　unscrupulous person.
snooperscope
snootful
snotnosed
snowball (n., v.)
snowbank
snowbelt
snowbird
snow-blind (adj.)
snow blindness
snow blower
snow board (Sports)
snowbound
snowcap/snowcapped
snow cover
snowdrift
snowfall
snow fence
snow guard
snow job
snow line
snowmaking
snowman
snowmelt
snowmobile
snowpack
snowplow
snowscape
snowshoe
snowslide
snowstorm
snowsuit
snow thrower
snow tire
snow train
snow under (v.)
snow-white (adj.)
snub-nosed
snuffbox
so-and-so (n.; pl.
　so-and-sos)

soapbox
soap bubble
soap flakes
soap opera
soap powder
soapstone
soapsuds
S.O.B. (sometimes lower-
　case)
sober-headed
sober-minded
sobersided
sobersides
sob-sister
sob story
so-called
soccer mom
social climber
social-minded
social register
social secretary
social security (sometimes
　capped)
social service
social work
sociobiology
sociocultural
socioeconomics
sock away (v.)
socked-in (adj.)
sockeroo
sock-in (v.)
Socratic method
soda cracker
soda fountain
soda jerk
soda pop
soda water
sodbuster
sodium-vapor lamp
sofa bed
so far as

softback: Paperback.
softball/softballer
soft-boiled
softbound: Paperback.
soft coal
soft copy (Computers)
soft-core
softcover: Paperback.
soft drink
soft drug
soft focus (Photography)
soft-focus (adj.)
soft goods
soft ground (Etching)
softheaded
softhearted
softkey (Computers)
soft-land (v.)
soft landing (Economics)
soft lens
soft line
soft-liner (n.)
soft news
soft pedal (n.)
soft-pedal (v.)
soft porn/soft pornography
soft rock
soft-rock geology
soft sell (n.)
soft-sell (v., adj.)
soft-shell (adj.)
soft-shoe (n., adj.)
soft shoulder
soft soap (n.)
soft-soap (v.)
soft-soaper
soft-spoken
soft spot
soft-top (n., adj.)
soft touch
software
softwood

soil bank
soil binder
soilborne
soil pipe
solar cell
solar day
solar energy
solar heat (n.)
solar-heat (v.)
solar house/solar home
solar mass
solar month
solar plexus
solar power
solar system
solar wind
solar year
soldier of fortune
soldiers' home
sold-out (adj.)
soleplate (Carpentry)
soleprint
solid angle
solid-looking
Solid South
solid-state (adj., Electronics)
so long
someday (adv.): "Someday I'll find you, at some day in the future."
someplace (adv.): "It's someplace around here. It's in some place nearby."
somersault
sometime (adv.): "Sometime we'll know, at some time in the future." "We must spend some time on it sometime soon." "It was some time ago."
sometimes (adv.): Now and then.

someway (adv.): In some way; somehow.
song and dance [Hyphenate as adj.]
songfest
songsmith
songwriter
sonic boom
son-in-law
son of a bitch (pl. sons of bitches)
soothsay (v.)
soothsayer/soothsaying
sorehead
sore throat
so-so
sotto voce (It.)
soul food
soul mate
soul music
soul-searching
soundalike (n.)
sound-and-light show
sound barrier
sound bite
sound block
sound board: Sounding board.
soundbox
sound effect
sound head (Movies)
sound hole (Music)
sounding board
soundman
sound off (v.)
soundproof
sound stage
soundtrack
sound truck
sound wave
soup-and-fish: A man's formal evening dress.

soupbone
soup du jour (F.)
soup kitchen
soup plate
soupspoon
soup-to-nuts (adj.)
sourball
source book
sour cream
sourdough (n., adj.)
sour grapes
sour mash
sourpuss
sous chef
southbound
southeast/southeastern
southeast by east
southeast by south
southeaster
southeasterly
southeasterner
southeastward/ southeastwardly
southerner
southernmost
southland
southpaw
South Pole
south-southeast/ south-southeastward
south-southwest/ south-southwestward
southward/southwardly
southwest by south
southwest by west
southwester
southwesterly
southwesterner
southwestward/ southwestwardly
sou'wester: Waterproof hat; oilskin slicker.

sowbelly
soybean
soy flour
soy sauce
Space Age
space-age (adj.)
spaceband (Printing)
space bar
spaceborne
space capsule
space charge
spacecraft
spaced-out
spaceflight
space heater/space heating
Spacelab
space law
spaceless
spaceman
space mark (Printing)
spaceport
space probe
space rate
space-saving
spaceship
spaceshot
space shuttle
space station
space suit
space-time continuum
   (Physics)
space walk (n.)
space-walk (v.)
spaceward
spacewoman
space writer
spadework
spaghetti strap
spareribs
spare tire
spark chamber
sparkover (n.)

spark plug (n.)
sparkplug (v.)
sparring partner
speakeasy
speakerphone
speaking in tongues
speaking tube
spear-carrier
spearhead
spearman
spearpoint
special agent
special court-martial
special effects
special-interest group
special-order (v.)
spectator sport
spectrochemical
spectrochemistry
spectroheliograph
spectrophotometer
speechmaker
speech recognition
speechwriter
speedball
speedboat/speedboating
speed bump
speed demon
speed freak
speed limit
speed-read (v.)
speed-reading
speed shop
speed skating
speed trap
speedup (n.)
speedwalk (n.)
speedway
speedwriting
spellbind/spellbinder
spellbound
spell checker (Computers)

spelldown: A spelling competition.
spelling bee
spendthrift
sperm bank
sperm cell
sperm oil
sperm whale
spick-and-span
spider web (n.)
spiderweb (v.)
spike heel
spillback (n.)
spillover (n.)
spillproof
spillway
spina bifida
spinal column/spinal cord
spindle file
spindlelegs
spindleshanks
spin doctor
spindrift
spin-dry (v.)
spinmeister
spinnaker (Nautical)
spinning wheel
spin-off (n.)
spinout (n.)
spinproof
spin the bottle: A kissing game.
spiral-bound
spit and image
spit and polish
spitball
spit curl
spite fence
spitfire
spit in the ocean (Cards)
spitting image
splashboard

splash dam
splashdown
splayfoot (n., adj.)
splayfooted
splendiferous
splint bone
split-brain (adj.)
split decision
split-dollar insurance
split end
split-fingered fastball (Baseball)
split flap (Aeronautics)
split image range finder
split-level (n., adj.)
split-off (n.)
split page (Newspapers)
split rail
split roll (Economics)
split run: A pressrun.
split screen
split second
split shift
splitsville
split ticket
split-up (n.)
spoil bank (Mining)
spoilsport
spoils system
spokesman/spokeswoman
spokesperson
sponge bath
sponge cake
sponge rubber
spoon bread
spoondrift
spoonerism
spoon-fed (adj.)
spoon-feed (v.)
sport fish
sportfisherman
sportfishing

sporting chance
sporting house
sports car
sportscast/sportscasting
sport shirt/sport jacket
sportsman
sportsmanship
sportswear
sportswoman
sportswriter
spot announcement
spot check (n.)
spot-check (v.)
spotlight
spot line (Theater)
spot market
spot meter
spot news
spot pass (Basketball,
    Football)
spot price
spot test (n.)
spot-test (v.)
spraddle-legged (adj., adv.)
spray can
spray-dart (v.)
spray gun
spray paint (n.)
spray-paint (v.)
spray tank
spread eagle (n.)
spread-eagle (adj., v.)
spreader beam
spreader-ditcher (Railroad)
spreadsheet
springboard
spring chicken
spring-clean (v.)
spring-cleaning (n.)
spring fever
springhead
springhouse

spring lamb
spring-load (v.)
spring-loaded (adj.)
spring lock
spring tide
springtime
springwater
spruce-up (n.)
spunbonded (adj.)
spun-bonding (n.)
spun glass
spun rayon/spun silk
spun sugar
spun yarn (n., Nautical)
spur-of-the-moment (adj.)
spur track (Railroad)
spyglass
spymaster
squad car
squad room
squadsman
squall line
square dance/
    square dancing
square-dance (v.)
square deal
squarehead
square knot
square-law (adj.,
    Electronics)
square one: Something to go
    back to.
square-rigged (Nautical)
square-rigger
square root
square sail (Nautical)
square shooter
square-shouldered
squaresville
square-toed
squatter's right
squawk box

squeaky-clean
squeegee
squeeze bottle
squeezebox
squeeze play (Baseball)
squint-eyed
squirrel cage
squirt can/squirt gun
stablemate
stab wound
stackup (n., Aviation)
stagecoach
stagecraft
stage door
stage-door Johnny
stage fright
stagehand
stage left/stage right
stage-manage (v.)
stage manager
stage set
stagestruck
stage whisper
staging area
stag party
stained glass
staircase
StairMaster™
stairstep
stairway/stairwell
stakeholder
stakeout (n.)
stalemate
stalking-horse
stamping ground
stamp mill
stamp tax
stand-alone (adj., n.;
  Computers)
standard-bearer
Standardbred (breed of
  horse)

standard-bred (adj.)
Standard English
standard of living
standby
stand-down (Military)
stand-in (n.)
standing broad jump
  (Track)
standing order
standing room
standoff (n., adj.)
standoffish
standout (n., adj.)
standpat (n., adj.)
standpatter
standpipe
standpoint
standstill
stand-up (adj.)
Stanford-Binet test
starboard
star-chamber (adj.)
star-crossed
star cut (Gems)
star drill
stardust
stare decisis (L.)
starfish
starflower
stargaze (v.)
stargazer
starquake (Astronomy)
star route
starry-eyed
star-shaped (adj.)
Star-Spangled Banner
star-studded
star system
starting block (Track)
starting gate
start-up (n., adj.)
star turn (Theater)

state aid
statecraft
statehouse
state of the art
state of war
stateroom
state's attorney
stateside (adj., adv.)
statesider
statesman
statesmanship
states' righter
states' rights
statewide
static cling
station break
station house
stationmaster
stations of the cross
station-to-station
station wagon
status group
status quo
status symbol
statute of limitations
stay-at-home (n., adj.)
staybolt
steady-going
steady-handed
steakhouse
steak knife
steam bath
steamboat
steam boiler
steamfitter
steam hammer
steam heat
steam-heated (adj.)
steam iron
steampipe
steamroller (n., v., adj.)
steamship

steam shovel
steam table
steel band (Music)
steel-faced
steel gray
steel guitar
steelmaker/steelmaking
steel mill
steel trap
steel wool
steelwork(s)
steelworker
steelyard
steeplechase (n., v.)
steeplechasing
steeplejack
steering gear
steering wheel
stem turn (Skiing)
stemware
stemwinder
stemwinding
Stenograph™
stenotype (formerly a
   trademark)
stenotypy
stepbrother
step-by-step (adj., adv.)
stepchild
step cut (Jewelry)
stepdance
stepdaughter
step-down (adj., Electricity)
stepfather
step function (Mathematics)
step-in (n., adj.)
stepladder
stepmother
step-off (n.)
step-on (adj.)
stepparent
stepped-up (adj.)

stepping-off place
steppingstone
step rocket
stepsister
stepson
step turn (Skiing)
step-up (adj., n.)
stepwise (adv., adj.)
sternward
sternwheel (n., Nautical)
stern-wheel (adj.)
sternwheeler (n.)
stewbum
stewpan/stewpot
stick-at-it-ive
stickball
stick-built
sticker price
stick figure
stickhandle (v., Sports)
stickhandler/stickhandling
sticking place
sticking point
stick-in-the-mud
stick-on (n.)
stickout (n., adj.)
stickpin
stick shift
stick-to-it-ive (adj.)
stick-to-it-iveness
stickum
stickup
sticky fingers
sticky wicket
stiff-arm (adj.)
stiff-necked
stiff upper lip
still and all
stillbirth/stillborn
still hunt (n.)
still-hunt (v.)
still life [Hyphenate as adj.]

Stillson wrench™
still water
stinkaroo or stinkeroo
stink bomb
stinkpot
stir-crazy
stir-fried (adj.)
stir-fry (n., adj., v.)
stock book
stockboy
stockbreeder/stockbreeding
stockbroker
stock buyback
stock car
stock certificate
stock clerk
stock exchange
stock farm
stock guard (Railroad)
stockholder
stockholder of record
stocking cap
stocking feet
stocking stuffer
stock in trade
stockjobber
stockkeeper
stockman
stock market
stock option
stockout (n.)
stockpile
stockpot
stock power
stockroom
stock split
stock-still (adj.)
stocktaking
stockyard
stomachache
stomachy
Stone Age

stone-blind
stone-broke
stone-cold
stonecutter
stone-dead
stone-deaf
stoneface
stone-ground
stonemason
stone's throw
stonewall (v., adj.)
stonewaller/stonewalling
stoneware
stonewash
stony-faced
stonyhearted
stool pigeon
stop-and-go (adj.)
stopcock
stopgap
stoplight
stop-loss (adj.)
stop-loss clause (Insurance)
stop motion (Movies)
stop-off (n.)
stop order
stop-out (n.)
stopover (n.)
stop payment (n.)
stop sign
stop street
stop volley (Tennis)
stopwatch
store-bought
store brand
storefront
storehouse
storekeeper
storeowner
storeroom
storewide
stormbound

storm cellar
storm center
storm coat
storm door
storm house
stormproof
storm sewer
storm signal
storm surge
storm track
storm trooper/storm
   troops
storm warning/storm
   watch
storm window
storyboard (Movies, TV)
storybook
story line
storyteller/storytelling
storywriter
stouthearted/
   stoutheartedly
stoutheartedness
stovepipe hat
stovetop
stowaway (n.)
straddle truck
straight A
straight-ahead (adj.)
straight and narrow
straight angle
straight-arm (v., n.;
   Football)
straight arrow
straightaway (adj., adv.)
straight-backed (adj.)
straight chain (n.,
   Chemistry)
straightedge (n.)
straight face
straight-faced (adj.)
straight flush (Poker)

straightforward (adj., adv.)
straight-from-the-shoulder (adj.)
straight-line (adj.)
straight man (Entertainment)
straight matter (Printing)
straight-out (adj.)
straight poker
straight razor
straight shooter
straight ticket (Politics)
straight time
straitjacket
strait-laced
stranglehold
straphang (v.)
straphanger
straw boss (n.)
straw-boss (v.)
straw-hat (adj.)
straw man
straw vote
streambed
streamline (n., v.)
streamlined
stream of consciousness [Hyphenate as adj.]
streetcar
street fighter
streetlight
street name (Stock Exchange)
street people
streetsmart (adj.)
street smarts (n.)
streetwalker
streetwise (adj.)
streetworker
strep throat
stress mark
stress test (n.)

stress-test (v.)
stretcher-bearer
stretch mark
stretchout (n.)
strike benefit
strikebound
strikebreaker/ strikebreaking
strike fault (Geology)
strikeout (Baseball)
strikeover
strike zone (Baseball)
striking price (Finance)
string bag
string bean
stringboard
stringcourse (Architecture)
stringholder
string line (Billiards, Pool)
stringpiece (Building)
string quartet
string tie
strip bond (Finance)
strip chart
strip city: Pertaining to urban development.
strip-crop (v.)
strip-cropping
strip farm
striplight (Theater)
strip mall
strip map
strip-mine (v.)
strip mining
stripped-down (adj.)
strip poker
strip search (n.)
strip-search (v.)
strip steak
striptease (n., v.)
stripteaser
strobe light

151

stroke hole (Golf)
stroke play (Golf)
strong-arm (adj., v.)
strongbox
stronghold
strongman
strong-minded
strong point
strongroom
strong safety (Football)
strong side (Football)
strong suit
strong-willed
strung-out (adj.)
stuccowork
stuck-up (adj.)
studbook
studdingsail (Nautical)
stud fee
studhorse
studio couch
stud poker
studwork
study group
study hall
stuffed shirt
stumblebum
stumbling block
stump farm
stump speech
stun gun
stuntman/stuntwoman
stylebook
style sheet

NOTE: All words in our dictionaries with the prefix *sub-* (except for those containing a capitalization, *sub-Andean, sub-Christian,* e.g.) are written solid. Some examples follow:

subagent
subbasement
subconscious
subcontinent
subcontract
subfloor
subfreezing
subgroup
subhuman
submachine gun
subnormal
subordinate
subornation of perjury
subplot
subpoena duces tecum (L.)
sub-rosa (L., adj.)
sub-Saharan
substandard
subtopic
subtropical

such and such
suchlike
sucker bait
suction cup
suction pump
sudden death
sudden infant death syndrome (SIDS)
sugar beet
sugar bowl
sugar-candy (adj.)
sugarcane
sugarcoat (v.)
sugarcoating (n.)
sugar daddy
sugar-free
sugarhouse
sugarloaf
sugarplum
sugar spoon

sugar tongs
sui generis (L.)
sui juris (L.)
suitcase
suit-dress
sukiyaki (Japanese cookery)
sulfa drug
sum and substance
summa cum laude (L.)
summary court-martial
summary judgment
summer camp
summerhouse
summer school
summer solstice
summer stock (Theater)
summertime
sump pump
sum total
sum-up (n.)
sunback
sunbaked
sunbath
sunbathe
sunblock
sunbonnet
sunbow
sunbreak
sunburn
sunburst
sun-cured
sun dance
Sunday-go-to-meeting (adj.)
Sunday punch (Boxing)
Sunday school
sun deck
sundial
sun disk
sundog
sundown
sundowner: An alcoholic
  drink.

sundress
sun-dried
sunfast
sun gear (Machinery)
sunglasses
sunglow
sun god
sunken garden
sunlamp
sunlight/sunlit
sunny side
sunny-side up
sun parlor
sun porch
sunproof
sunrise service
sunroof
sunroom
sunscreen
sunseeker
sunset law
sunshade
sunshine law
sunsick
sunsign (Astrology)
sunspot
sunstone
sunstroke
sunstruck
sunsuit
suntan (n., v.)
suntanned
suntans (military uniforms)
sunup
sun visor
sunward
sunwise
suo jure (L.)

NOTE: Almost without exception, all words with the prefix
super- are written solid.

super band
Super Bowl
supercool (v., adj.)
super-duper
superego
super giant slalom (Skiing)
superhighway
superiority complex
supernova (Astronomy)
supernumerary
superstar
superstore
supper club
suppertime
supply-side (adj.)
supply-sider (n.)
support level (Stock
  Market)
support price
supranational
sure-enough (adj.)
sure enough (adv.)
surefire
surefooted
sure-handed
sure thing
surface-active agent
  (Chemistry)
surface-ripened (of cheese)
surface-to-air missile
surface-to-underwater
surf and turf
surfboard
surfboarder/surfboarding
surf boat
surf casting
surfriding
surge protector
surprise party
surreal
surrealism
surrebuttal

surrogate mother
surtax
survey course
survival kit
survivor guilt
suspense account
suspension bridge
sustained-release
  (Chemistry)
swage block
swagger coat
swagger stick
swallowtail
swallow-tailed coat
swamp buggy
swamp fever
swamp gas
swampland
swan boat
swan dive (n.)
swan-dive (v.)
swansdown
swan's neck: An S curve.
swan song
swashbuckle (v.)
swashbuckler/
  swashbuckling
swash plate (Machinery)
swayback
swaybacked
swearing-in
swearword
sweatband
sweatbox
sweat equity
sweatercoat
sweater girl
sweat gland
sweatpants
sweatshirt
sweatshop
sweat socks

sweat suit
sweep account (Finance)
sweepback (Aeronautics)
sweep check (Ice Hockey)
sweep hand (Horology)
sweep-second
sweepstakes
sweet-and-sour (adj.)
sweetbread
sweetheart contract
sweetie pie
sweetmeat
sweet roll
sweet-scented
sweet talk (n.)
sweet-talk (v.)
swell box (of a pipe organ)
swellhead (n.)
swellheaded (adj.)
sweptback (Aeronautics)
sweptwing (Aeronautics)
swift-footed
swimming hole
swimming pool
swimsuit
swimwear
swindle sheet
swingback (n.)
swing bridge
swing by (n., Aerospace)
swinging door
swing loan
swingman
swingover
swing shift
swing-wing (n., Aeronautics)
switchback
switchblade
switchboard
switchbox
switched-on (adj.)
switch engine (Railroad)

switcheroo
switchgear (Electricity)
switch-hit (v., Baseball)
switch-hitter
switch knife
switchman
switch-off (n.)
switch-on (n.)
switchover (n.)
switch plate
switchyard
swivel chair
swivel gun
swivel-hipped
swizzle stick
swordcraft
sword dance
swordplay
swordsman
swung dash: Punctuation
  mark.
symbiosis
sympathy strike
synchro unit (Electricity)
synecdoche
syntax
system program
  (Computers)
systems software
  (Computers)

T

tab key
table d'hôte (F.)
table-hop (v.)
tablespoonful
table stake (Poker)
table talk
table tennis
tabletop

tableware
table wine
tabula rasa (L.)
tackboard
tack hammer
tack room
ta-da
tagalong
tagboard
tag boat
tag day
tag end
tag line
tag, rag, and bobtail
tag sale
tag team (Wrestling)
tailback (Football)
tailboard
tailbone
tail cone (Rocketry)
tail end
tailfirst
tailgate
tailgater
taillight
tailor-made
tailpiece
tailpipe
tail plane
tailrace (Mining)
tail skid (Aeronautics)
tailspin
tailstock
tailwind
take-along (adj., n.)
take-away (n., adj.)
takeback (n., adj.)
take-charge (adj.)
takedown (n., adj.)
take-home pay
take-in (n.)
takeoff (n.)

takeout (n., adj.)
takeover (n.)
take-up (n.)
take-up reel (Movies)
talebearer/talebearing
talent scout
taleteller
talkathon
talk-back (Radio and TV)
talkfest
talking book
talking head
talking point
talking-to (n.)
talk show
tall drink
tall one (drink)
tallyho
tallyman
Tammany Hall
tam-o'-shanter
tamperproof
tank car
tank destroyer
tanked up: Drunk.
tank farm
tankship
tank suit
tank top
tank town
tank trailer
tank truck
tap dance (n.)
tap-dance (v.)
tap dancer/tap dancing
tape deck
tape drive (Computers)
tape editing
tapeman (Surveying)
tape measure
tape player
tape-record (v.)

tape recorder/
   tape recording
taper off (v.)
tapeworm
taphole
taproom
taproot
tap water
tar baby
tar ball
target date
tarpaper
tarpit
tartar sauce
task force
taskmaster/taskmistress
taste bud
tastemaker
tatterdemalion
tattersall
tattletale
tattletale gray
tax base
tax bracket
tax-bracket creep
tax-deductible
tax deed
tax-deferred annuity
tax-exempt
tax-free
tax haven
taxi dancer
taximeter
taxi stand
taxiway (Airport)
tax-paid (adj.)
taxpayer
tax rate
tax return
tax sale
tax shelter
tax stamp

T-bill
T-bone steak
T cell
tea bag
teach-in (n.)
teaching aid
teacup
tea dance
tea garden
tea gown
teahouse
teakettle
teammate
team play/team player
teamwork
tea party
teapot
tearaway (adj., n.)
tear bomb
teardown (n.)
teardrop
tear gas (n.)
tear-gas (v.)
tearjerker
tear-jerking
tear-off (adj.)
tearoom
tear-out (adj.)
tear sheet
tear-stained
tear strip
teary-eyed
teataster
teatime
tea tray
tea wagon
technical knockout
teddy bear
teddy boy (Brit.)
teeing ground (Golf)
teenage/teenager
teensy-weensy

teenybopper
teeny-weeny
tee shirt: T-shirt.
teeterboard
teetertotter
teetotal/teetotaler
teevee: TV.
te-hee (n., v., interjec.)
telecamera
telecast
telecom
telecommute
telecommuting
teleconference
Telecopier™
telecourse
teledrama
telefeature
telefilm
telemark (Skiing)
telemarketing
Telephoto™: Apparatus for
   electrical transmission of
   photographs.
telephoto (adj.)
telephoto lens
teleplay
teleprinter
TelePrompTer™
telescope/telescopy
telescreen
teleshopping
teletext (TV)
telethon
Teletype™
teletypewriter
teleview (v.)
telex
tell-all (adj.)
telltale
Telstar™
temper tantrum

tempest-tossed
tenancy in common (Law)
tenant farmer
ten-cent store
ten code (Radio)
tenderfoot
tenderhearted
tender offer
tenfold
ten-four (CB radio slang)
ten-gallon hat
10-gauge shotgun
tennis elbow
tenor clef (Music)
tenpenny nail
ten percenter: An agent.
tenpins
tensile strength
ten-speed (n., adj.)
ten-spot
ten-strike
tent circus
tent dress
tenterhooks
tentmaker
tent show
tent stitch
tent trailer
tepee
teriyaki (Japanese cookery)
term paper
term policy (Insurance)
terra cotta
terra firma (L.)
terror-stricken
terry cloth
test ban
test case
testcross (Genetics)
test-drive (v.)
test flight
test-fly (v.)

test paper
test pattern (TV)
test pilot
test tube (n.)
test-tube baby
tête-à-tête (F.; n., adj., adv.)
Texas leaguer (Baseball)
Tex-Mex
textbook
textbookish
text editor (Computers)
thanksgiver
thankworthy
thank-you (n., adj.)
thank-you-ma'am: A bump in the road.
thataway
theatergoer
theater-in-the-round
theater of the absurd
theater of war
thé dansant (F.)
theftproof
theme park
theme song
thenceforth/thenceforward
thereabout(s)
thereafter
thereat
thereby
therefor
therefore
therefrom
therein
thereinafter
thereinto
thereof
thereon
thereto
theretofore
thereunder
thereupon

therewith
therewithal
thick and thin
thickhead/thickheaded
thickset
thick-skinned
thick-witted
thighbone
thingamabob/thingamajig
thing-in-itself (n.)
thinking cap
think tank
thin-layer chromatography
thin-skinned
third base/third baseman
third class (n.)
third-class (adj., adv.)
third degree (n.)
third-degree (adj., v.)
third-degree burn
third dimension
third ear/third eye: Intuition.
third estate
thirdhand (adj., adv.)
third mate
third party
third-party software (Computers)
third person (Grammar)
third position (Ballet)
third rail (Railroads)
third-rate (adj.)
third-rater
third-stream (adj., Music)
Third World
30-dash (Printing, Journalism)
.30-30 (Firearms)
thisaway
thistledown
this-worldliness

thitherto
thoroughbred
thoroughfare
thoroughgoing
thought disorder
thought-out (adj.)
thought transference
threadbare
thread mark
three-bagger (Baseball)
three-base hit
three-card monte
three-color
three-cornered
3-D or three-D
three-decker
three-dimensional
threefold
three-gaited
three-handed
three-legged
three-legged race
three-master (Nautical)
three-mile limit
three of a kind
three-peat (v.): To win a
third consecutive victory.
three-phase
three-piece (adj.)
three-ply (adj.)
three-point landing
three-quarter(s) (adj.)
three-quarter time
three-ring circus
three R's
threescore
threesome
three-speed (n., adj.)
three-square (adj.)
three-star (adj.)
three-wheeler
threshing machine

threshold
thrift shop
throttlehold
throughput
through street
through-the-lens meter
throughway: Variant of
thruway.
throwaway
throwback
throw-in (n.)
throw weight (Ballistic
Missiles)
thruway
thumbhole
thumb index
thumbnail
thumbprint
thumbscrew
thumbs-down (n.)
thumb-sucker
thumbs-up (n.)
thumbtack
thunderbolt
thunderclap
thundercloud
thunderhead (Meteorology)
thundershower/
thundersquall
thunderstorm
thunderstricken
thunderstrike (v.)
thunderstroke
thunderstruck
tick-borne
ticker tape
ticker-tape parade
ticket agent/ticket agency
ticket office
ticket scalper
tick fever
tickler coil

tickler file
ticktack
tick-tack-toe
ticktock
ticky-tacky (n., adj.)
tidal basin
tidal benchmark
tidal wave
tidbit
tiddlywinks
tide-bound
tide gage
tide gate
tidehead
tideland
tidemark
tide table
tidewater
tideway
tieback
tie beam
tiebreaker
tie clasp/tie clip
tie-down (n.)
tie-dye (v.)
tie-dyeing
tie-in (adj., n.)
tie line
  (Telecommunications)
tiepin
tie plate (Railroad)
tie plug (Railroad)
tie rod
tie silk
tie tack
tie-up (n.)
tight end (Football)
tight-fisted
tightfitting
tight-knit (adj.)
tight-lipped/tight-mouthed
tightrope

tight spot
tightwad
tightwire
tilt-top table
tilt-up (adj., Building Trades)
timberhead (Nautical)
timber hitch (n.)
timberhitch (v.)
timberjack/timberman
timberland
timberline
timber mill
timber wolf
timberwork
time and a half
time and motion study
time-binding
time bomb
time capsule
timecard
time chart
time clock
time-consuming
time deposit (Banking)
timed-release, also
  time-release (adj.)
time exposure
time frame
time-honored
time immemorial
timekeeper
time killer
time lag
time-lapse (adj.)
time-lapse photography
time limit
time loan
time lock
time machine
time-out (n.; pl. time-outs)
time out of mind
timepiece

timesaver/timesaving
time-share (n., v.)
time-sharing
time sheet
timespan
time stamp
timetable
time-tested
time warp
timework/timeworker
timeworn
time zone
tinderbox
tin ear
tinfoil
ting-a-ling
tin god
tin hat
tinhorn
tinker's damn
Tinkertoy™
tin lizzie
Tin Pan Alley
tin plate (n.)
tin-plate (v.)
Tinseltown: Hollywood.
tinsmith
tin soldier
tintinnabulation
tintype
tinware
tip-in (Basketball)
tip-off
tip of the iceberg
tip sheet
tiptoe
tiptop (n., adj.)
tissue paper
tissue typing
tit for tat
tittle-tattle (n., v.)
T-man

to-and-fro (n., adj.)
to and fro (adv.): "The busy
    to-and-fro of the holiday
    shoppers seemed to have
    a to-and-fro motion, as
    people walked to and fro."
toastmaster/toastmistress
to-be (adj.)
to-do (n.; pl. to-dos)
toe box
toecap
toe dance (n.)
toe-dance (v.)
toehold
toe-in (n.)
toe loop (Skating)
toe-out (n.)
toeplate
toe-to-toe (adj., adv.)
toggle bolt/toggle joint
toggle switch
toilet powder
toilet-train (v.)
toilet training (n.)
toilet water
toilworn
to-ing and fro-ing
tollbooth
toll bridge
toll call
toll collector
toll-free (adj., adv.)
tollgate
tollgatherer
tollhouse
toll road
tomahawk
Tom and Jerry
tomboy
tombstone
tomcat (n., v.)
Tom Collins

Tom, Dick, and Harry
tomfoolery
tommy gun (n.)
tommy-gun (v.)
tommyrot
tom-tom
tone cluster (Music)
tone control
tone-deaf
tone deafness
tone dialing
tone painting
tone poem
tone-up (n.)
tongue-and-groove joint
tongue depressor
tongue-in-cheek (adj.)
tongue in cheek (adv.)
tongue-lash (v.)
tongue-lashing
tongue-tie (n., v.)
tongue-tied (adj.)
tongue twister
tonguing-and-grooving
  plane (Carpentry)
tonic water
ton-mile
toolbox
toolhouse
toolmaker
toolroom/toolshed
tool steel
toothache
tooth and nail
toothbrushing
tooth fairy
toothpaste
toothpick
tooth powder
toothsome
too-too (adj., adv.)
tootsy-wootsy

top banana
top billing
top brass
topcoat
top dog
top dollar
top-down (Computers)
top drawer [Hyphenate as
  adj.]
top-dress (v.)
top dressing (n.)
top flight (n.)
topflight or top-flight (adj.)
top gun
top hat [Hyphenate as adj.]
top-heavy
top kick: First sergeant.
topknot
topless
top-level (adj.)
topline (adj.)
top loader
toplofty
topman (Nautical)
topmast
topmost
topnotch
top-of-the-line (adj.)
topotype (Biology)
top round
topsail
topsail schooner
top-secret (adj.)
top sergeant
topside(s) (n., adj., adv.)
topsider
topsoil
topspin (Sports)
topstitch (v., n.)
topsy-turvy/topsy-turvydom
top ten
top timber

torchbearer
torchlight
torch singer/torch song
tornado belt
torpedo boat
torpedoman
torque converter
torque wrench
Torrid Zone
torsion bar
torsion group
torso murder
tortfeasor (Law)
tortoiseshell
tosspot
tossup
total eclipse
total recall
tote bag
tote board
tote box
totem pole
touch and go [Hyphenate
  as adj.]
touch football
touchhole (Firearms)
touchline (Rugby, Soccer)
touchmark
touch paper
touch plate
touchscreen (Computers)
touchstone
touch system
touch-tone (adj., n.)
touch-type (v.)
touch-up
tough love
tough-minded
tour de force (F.)
touring car
tourist class
tourist court

tourist home
tourist trap
tour of duty
tout de suite (F.)
towaway
tow bar
towboat
towhead
tow-headed
to wit
towline
town car
town clerk
town crier
town hall
townhome
town house
town meeting
township
townsman/townspeople/
  townswoman
town-wear
towpath
towrope
tow truck
toxic shock syndrome
toxin-antitoxin
  (Immunology)
toy dog
toymaker
toyshop
trace element
tracer bullet
tracing paper
tracing tape
track and field [Hyphenate
  as adj.]
trackball (Computers)
track brake
tracking shot (Movies, TV)
tracking station
tracking system

tracklayer
track lighting
trackman
track meet
track record
track shoe
trackside
track spike
track suit
track system
track-train dynamics
trackwalker
trackway
tract house
traction engine
tractor feed (Computers)
tractor-trailer
trade acceptance
trade association
trade barrier
trade book
trade council
trade discount
trade edition
trade-in (n., adj.)
trademark
trade name (n.)
trade-name (v.)
trade-off
trade paper
trade paperback
trade route
trade school
trade secret
trade show
tradesman/tradespeople/
    tradeswoman
trade union
trade unionism
trade wind
trading post
trading stamp

traffic circle
traffic cop
traffic court
traffic engineering
traffic island
traffic jam
traffic light
traffic manager
traffic pattern
tragicomedy
trail bike
trailblaze (v.)
trailblazer
trailboard (Nautical)
trailer camp
trailer car (Railroad)
trailer park
trail head
trainbearer
training aid
training pants
training school
training wall
training wheels
trainline
trainload
trainman/trainmaster
trainsick
tram-car
tramroad
tramway
transatlantic
transceiver
transcendental meditation
transcriptase (Biochemistry)
transcurrent
transfer agent
transpersonal
transship
trapdoor
trapeze artist
trapshooting

trap shot (Sports)
trash can
trash fish
trashman
trash rack
trauma center
travel agency/travel agent
traveler's check
traveling bag
traveling-wave tube
 (Electronics)
travel shot (Movies, TV)
travel time
traverse rod
tray table
treadmill
treasure house
treasure hunt
treasure-trove
Treasury bill/Treasury bond
treble clef (Music)
treble staff (Music)
tree farm
tree-form frame
tree house
tree line: Timberline.
treelined
tree-surgeon
tree surgery
treetop
trelliswork
trench coat
trench foot
trench knife
trench mouth
trench warfare
trendline
trendsetter/trendsetting
trestle table
trestletree (Nautical)
trestlework
trial and error

trial balance
trial balloon
trial court
trial docket
trial examiner
trial lawyer
trial marriage
trial run
triathlete
triathlon
triaxial
tribesman/tribespeople
trickle-down theory
trick or treat
trick-or-treat (v.)
tricolor
tricornered
tried-and-true (adj.)
trigger finger
trigger-happy
triggerman
trijet
trilinear
trilingual
trimonthly
triphammer
triple bond (Chemistry)
triple-decker
triple-digit
triple fugue (Music)
triple-header
triple jump (Track and
 Field)
triple play (Baseball)
triple point (Physics)
triple-space (v.)
triple threat
triple time (Music)
triple-tongue (Music)
tripmeter
tripwire
trisect

tristate
trivalve (adj., n.)
triweekly
Trojan horse
trolley bus
trolley car
trolley line
trompe l'oeil (F.)
troop carrier
troopship
trophy room
tropic of Cancer
tropic of Capricorn
troubled waters
troublemaker
trouble man
troubleproof
troubleshoot (v.)
troubleshooter (n.)
troublesome
trouble spot
troy weight
truant officer
truckdriver/truckman
truck farm
truckline
truckload
truck stop
truck tractor
truck trailer
true bill (Law)
true blue [Hyphenate as
    adj.]
trueborn/truebred
true course
true-false test
truehearted
true-life (adj.)
truelove (n.)
true north
true time
trump card

trumped-up (adj.)
trundle bed
trunkful
trunk line
trust account
trustbuster
trust deed
trust fund
trustworthy
truth-function (n., Logic)
truth or consequences
truth serum
truth-value (Logic)
tryout
trysail (Nautical)
trysail mast
try square
trysting place
T-shirt
T square
T-stop (Photography)
T-strap
tubal ligation
tube-nosed
tube pan
tube sock(s)
tube top
tuckaway table
tuck-point (v., Masonry)
tuck pointing
tugboat
tug of war
tumbledown (adj.)
tumble-dry
tumbleweed
tummy tuck
tuned-in
tunesmith
tune-up (n.)
tuning fork
tunnel effect
tunnel of love

tunnel vision
turbocharge (v.)
turbocharger
turbojet
turboprop
turbo-ramjet engine
turbosupercharger
turfskiing
turkey shoot
turkey trot (n.)
turkey-trot (v.)
Turkish bath
Turkish towel
turnabout (n.)
turnaround (n.)
turnbuckle
turncoat
turndown (n., adj.)
turned-on (adj.)
turn-in (n.)
turn indicator
turnkey
turnoff (n.)
turn-on (n.)
turnout (n.)
turnover
turnpike
turn signal
turntable
turnup (n.)
turnverein (G.): Athletic club.
turtledove
turtleneck
tut-tut
Tweedledum and
    Tweedledee
'tween deck (Nautical)
twelvefold
twelve-mile limit
twelve-tone row (Music)
twentyfold
twenty-something

twenty-twenty or 20/20
    (vision)
twice-born (Hinduism)
twice-laid
twice-told
twilight zone
twin bed
twin bill
twinborn (adj.)
twin-engine
twinighter (Baseball)
twin-screw (adj., Nautical)
twin-size
two-bagger/two-base hit
two-bit (adj.)
two bits
two-by-four (adj.)
two cents worth
two-color
two-cycle
two-dimensional
two-edged
two-faced
two-family house
two-fisted
two-fold
twofold purchase
    (Mechanics)
2,4-D
two-handed
twolegged
two-master (Nautical)
two-minute warning
    (Football)
two-name paper (Banking)
two-party system
two-phase (Electricity)
two-piece
two-ply
two-seater
two-sided
twosome

two-spot
two-star (adj.)
two-step (n., v.)
two-suiter (Bridge)
two-tier
two-time (v.)
two-time loser
two-timer (n.)
two-tone
two-track
two-way
two-wheeler
typecast (Theater)
type-cast (v., Printing)
typeface
typefounder
type-out (n.)
typescript
typeset (v., adj.)
typesetter/typesetting

U

U-boat
U bolt
UFO
uh-huh
ultima Thule (L.)

NOTE: Words with the prefix *ultra-* (even long ones like *ultramicrofiche*) are written solid. Exception: *ultra-abysmal.*

umpteen
umpteenth
umpty-umpth

NOTE: Unless combined with a proper noun or adjective (as in *un-American*, e.g.), words with the prefix *un-* are written solid.

uncalled-for
unclean hands (Law)
Uncle Sam
Uncle Tom
Uncle Tomism
undertow (n., but a ship is *under tow*, two words)
under way: Said of a ship in motion — or a project in the works.
undreamed-of (adj.)
un-English
un-European
unfair practice
unheard-of
unhoped-for
union buster
union card
union jack
union label
union-made
union scale
union shop
union suit
unisex/unisexual
unit card (Library Science)
unit circle (Mathematics)
unit cost
unit price
unlooked-for
unpaid-for
unputdownable
unself-conscious
unskilled labor
unwished-for
unwritten law
up-anchor
up-and-coming (adj.)

169

up-and-down (adj.)
up-and-up (adj.)
up-bow (Music)
upbringing
upcard (Poker)
upcharge
upchuck
up-close (adj.)
upcoming
upcountry
upcropping
up-front (adj., adv.)
upgrade
upland
upload (Computers)
upmanship
upmarket (adj.)
up-or-out (adj.)
upper case (n.)
uppercase (adj., v.)
upper class [Hyphenate as adj.]
upperclassman
upper crust
uppercut (n., v.)
upper deck
upper hand
upper house
uppermost
upriver (adj., adv.)
ups and downs
upscale (adj., v., n.)
upset price
upside down
upside-down cake
upstage (adj., adv., v., n.)
upstate
upsweep (n., v.)
upsy-daisy
uptake
up-tempo (Music)
uptight (adj.)

uptightness (n.)
uptime (n.)
up-to-date/
    up-to-the-minute
upwind
urban sprawl
user-friendly
use tax
U-turn (n., v.)
U-2: Spy plane.
U-value

V

vacuum bottle
vacuum cleaner
vacuum gauge
vacuum-pack/
    vacuum-packed
vacuum tube
vainglorious (adj.)
vainglory (n.)
valet parking
value-added tax
value date (Banking)
valued policy (Insurance)
valve-in-head engine
valve lifter
valve stem
Vandyke beard
vanity case
vanity plate
vanity press
van pool
vantage point
vapor barrier
vapor lock
vapor trail
vaporware (Computer jargon)
variable-pitch (adj.)

variable-rate (adj.)
varicolored
variegated
variety show
variety store
varisized
Varityper™
vat dye
vat-dyed
V-chip
V-E Day
veejay
Velcro™
velvet glove
venetian blind
venial sin
venture capital
verisimilar (adj.)
verisimilitude
vernal equinox
very high frequency/
    very low frequency
vestal virgin
vested interest
vest-pocket (adj.)
vest-pocket park
veto power
veto-proof
vice admiral
vice-admiralty
vice-chairman
vice-chancellor
vice-consul
vice-presidency
vice president
viceroy
vice squad
vice versa
vicious circle
video art
video camera
videocassette

videocassette recorder
videoconference/
    videoconferencing
videodisk
video display terminal
video game
video jockey (veejay)
videophone
videoporn
videorecord (v.)
videorecorder
videotape (n., v.)
videotape recorder
videotaping
Vienna sausage
Vietcong
Vietnam
viewfinder
viewpoint
vintage wine/vintage year
vinyl acetate
vinyl chloride
violinmaker
virtual reality
vis-à-vis (F.)
visiting nurse
vital force
vital signs
vitreous humor
V-J Day
V neck
vocal cords: Not *chords!*
vogue word
voice box
voice mail
voice-over
voiceprint
voice vote
voir dire (Law)
volleyball
volt-ampere
voltmeter

voodoo/voodooism
voodoo economics
votegetter
vouchsafe
vox pop./vox populi (L.)

W

wage earner
wage scale
wageworker
wagonload
wah-wah (adj., n.)
Wailing Wall
wainscot/wainscoting
waistband
waist-deep/waist-high
waistline
waiting game
waiting list
waiting period
waiting room
waitlist (v.)
waitperson
wake-up (n., adj.)
walkabout (n., Australian)
walkaround pay
walkathon
walkaway (n.)
walkdown (n., adj.)
walkie-talkie
walk-in (n., adj.)
walk-in closet
walking-around money
walking papers
walking stick
walking wounded
Walkman™
walk-off (n.)
walk of life
walk-on (n.)

walkout (n., adj.)
walkover (n.)
walk-through (n., adj.; Theater)
walk-up (n., adj.)
walkway
wallboard
wall box
wallcovering
walleyed
wallflower
wall hanging
wall-hung (adj.)
wall painting
wallpaper
wall plate
wall plug
wallposter (in China)
wall rock (Mining)
Wall Streeter
wall-to-wall (adj., adv., n.)
waltz time
Wanderjahr (G.)
wanderlust
wannabe or wannabee: Aspirant.
want ad
want list
war baby
war bonnet
war bride
war chest
war cloud
war crime(s)
war cry
war dance
ward heeler
wardrobe mistress
wardroom
warehouseman
warehouser
war game

warhead
warhorse
warlike
warlock: A male witch.
warlord
warm-blooded
warmdown (n.)
warmed-over
warmed-up
warmer-upper
warm front
warm-hearted
warmonger/warmongering
warm spot
warm spring
warm tone (Photography)
warmup
warning track (Baseball)
war of nerves
war paint
warp and woof
war party
warpath
warp knit
warp-knitted
warp-knitting
warplane
war powers
warrantee: One to whom a
   warrant is made. It's always
   a noun, never a verb.
warship
war story
war surplus
wartime
war-weary
war whoop
war zone
wash-and-wear (adj.)
washateria
washbasin
washboard (n., adj.)

washbowl/washcloth
washday
washdown (n.)
washed-out (adj.)
washed-up (adj.)
washer-dryer
washerwoman
wash goods
washin (n., Aeronautics)
washout
washrag
washroom
wash sale (Stock Market)
washstand
washtub (n.)
washup (n.)
wasp waist
wastebasket
wasteland
wastepaper
waste pipe
wastewater
watchband
watchcase
watch chain
watchdog
watchmaker
watchman
watch pocket
watchtower
watchword
water ballet
water-base paint
waterbath
waterbed
water bomb
waterborne
water boy
water carrier
water closet
watercolor (n., adj.)
water-cool (v.)

water cooler
watercourse
watercraft
water cure
water curtain
watered-down
water-fast
waterfinder
waterflood
waterfowl
waterfront
Watergate: White House political scandal.
water gate: A floodgate.
water gauge
water glass
water hammer
waterhead
water heater
water hole
watering hole/ watering place
water jacket (n.)
water-jacket (v.)
waterjet
water level
water line
waterlocked
waterlogged
water main
waterman
watermark
water meter
water nymph
water paint
waterpick
WaterPik™
water pipe
water pistol
water polo
waterpower
waterproof

waterproofing
water-repellent/ water-resistant
water right
watersaver
waterscape
watershed
waterside (n., adj.)
water ski (n.)
water-ski (v.)
water-skiing
watersoak (v.)
water softener
water-soluble
watersport
water spot (n.)
water-spot (v.)
waterspout
water supply/water system
water table
water taxi
watertight
water tower
water trap
water-tube boiler
water turbine
water vapor
water wagon
waterway
waterwheel
water wings
water witch
waterworks
waterworn
watt-hour: Unit of energy.
wattmeter
wave band (Radio and TV)
waveform (Physics)
wave front (Physics)
waveguide
wavelength
wave-off (n., Aeronautics)

wave of the future
wave theory
wave train (Physics)
wave trap (Radio)
wax museum
wax paper
waxworks
waybill
wayfarer
waylay
way of the future: Wave of the future.
way-out (adj.)
ways and means
wayside
way station
waywardness
weaker sex
weakhanded
weak-headed
weakhearted
weak-kneed
weakminded
weak side
weak sister
weak-willed
wearability
wear and tear
wearisome
wear-out (n.)
wearproof
weasel word
weatherability
weather-beaten
weatherboard
weather-bound
weather bureau
weathercast/weathercaster
weathercock
weather deck
weather eye
weather gauge

weatherglass
weatherize
weatherman
weather map
weatherperson
weatherproof
weatherproofer
weather-resistant
weather ship
weather strip (n.)
weather-strip (v.)
weather stripping
weather tide (Nautical)
weathertight
weather vane
weather-wise
weatherworn
webfoot
webfooted/webtoed
wedge heel
weed cutter
weedkiller
weekday/weekend
weekender
weekend warrior
weeklong
weeknight/weeknightly
weep hole (Building Trades)
weeping willow
weewee (n., v.)
weft-knitted
weft knitting
weigh-in (n.)
weight belt (Scuba Diving)
weight density
weighted mean (Statistics)
weight for age (Horse Racing)
weightlifter/weightlifting
weight-watcher
weirdo
welcome mat

welcome wagon
welfare state
well-acquainted
well-adjusted
well-advised
well-appointed
well-balanced
well-behaved
well-being
well-beloved
wellborn
well-bred
well-built
well-chosen
well-conditioned
well-connected
well-defined
well-developed
well-disposed
well-done
well-dressed
well-earned
well-established
well-favored
well-fed
well-fixed
well-formed
well-founded
well-groomed
well-grounded
well-handled
wellhead (n.)
well-heeled
wellhole
wellhouse
well-informed
well-intentioned
well-kept
well-knit
well-known (adj.): "As is
   well known, he is a
   well-known author."

well-made
well-mannered
well-meaning
wellness
well-nigh
well-off
well-oiled
well-ordered
wellpoint (Engineering,
   Building Trades)
well-preserved
well-read
well-rounded
well-set
well-spoken
wellspring
well-taken
well-thought-of
well-timed
well-to-do
well-turned
well-used
well-wisher
well-worn
welterweight
Weltschmerz (G.)
werewolf
westbound
west by north
west by south
Westerner
westernmost
west-northwest
west-northwestward
westwardly
wetability
wetback
wet bar
wet blanket
wet cell (Electricity)
wet dock (Nautical)
wet dream

wetlands
wet mop (n.)
wet-mop (v.)
wet nurse (n.)
wet-nurse (v.)
wet pack
wet pudding (Metallurgy)
wet strength (Papermaking)
wet suit (Skin Diving)
wetting agent
wet wash
whacked-out
whaleback (Nautical)
whaleboat
whalebone
whale oil
whangdoodle
wharf rat
whatchamacallit
what-do-you-call-it
whatever (pron., adj.)
USAGE NOTE: Some author-
  ities, including the *Oxford
  English Dictionary*, prefer
  what ever (two words). We
  prefer it as such in the
  phrase "What ever hap-
  pened to ... ."
what-if (n.)
whatnot (n.)
what's-his(her)-name
whatsis
whatsoever
what-you-may-call-it [See
  whatchamacallit, above,
  as it's more commonly
  pronounced.]
wheat bread
wheat cake
wheat germ
wheelbarrow race
wheelbase

wheelchair
wheeler-dealer
wheel horse
wheelhouse
wheel lock
wheelman
wheel of fortune
wheel of life (Buddhism)
wheelspin
wheelwork
wheelwright
when-issued
whensoever
whereabouts
whereas
whereat
whereby
wherefore (adv., n.)
whereof
whereon
whereupon
wherewithal
wheyface/wheyfaced
whiffletree
whim-wham(s)
whing-ding: Wing-ding.
whip-and-tongue graft
  (Horticulture)
whipcord
whipcracker
whip hand
whiplash
whippersnapper
whipping boy
whipping post
whipsaw
whipstitch
whirlabout
whirligig
whirling dervish
whirlpool
whirlybird

whisk broom
whistle-blower
whistle stop (n.)
whistle-stop (v., adj.)
whitebeard
white belt (Martial Arts)
white blood cell
white-bread (adj.)
whitecap
white-collar
white-collar crime
white dwarf (Astronomy)
white elephant
whiteface: A Hereford; a performer.
white-faced
white feather
white flag
white frost
white-glove (adj.)
white goods
white-haired
white hat: A virtuous hero.
whitehead: A small pimple.
white-headed
white heat
white hope
white-hot
white iron
white knight
white-knuckle(d) (adj.)
white lead
white lie
white light
white lightning: Moonshine.
white line
white list
white-livered
white man's burden
white market
white meat
white metal

white noise
whiteout (n.)
white pages
white paper
white plague
white-robed
white rot
white rust
white sale
white sauce
white slave
white slaver
white slavery
white-slaving
white space
white supremacy
white tie [Hyphenate as adj.]
white trash
whitewall
whitewash
Whitewater: Failed Arkansas land-development venture.
white water [Hyphenate as adj.]
white wine
whizbang [Hyphenate as adj.]
whiz kid
whodunit
whole blood
whole cloth
whole-grain
wholehearted
whole hog [Hyphenate as adj.]
whole-length
whole milk
whole note (Music)
whole step (Music)
whole-tone scale (Music)
whole-wheat
whomsoever

whoop-de-do
whoosis
whoremonger
whosoever
who's who
Who's Who (book)
wicketkeeper (Cricket)
wide-angle lens
wide-awake (adj.)
wideband (adj.)
wide-bodied
wide-body (plane)
wide-eyed
wide-mouthed
wide-open
wide-ranging
wide receiver (Football)
wide-screen
widespread
wide-spreading
widow's mite
widow's peak
widow's walk
Wiener schnitzel
wienerwurst
wiggle room
wigmaker
wigwag
wilco (Radio)
wild-and-woolly (adj.)
wild card
wildcat (n., adj., v.)
wildcat strike
wildcatter
wild-eyed
wildfire
wildflower
wildfowl
wild-goose chase
wild-headed
wildlife
wild man

wild pitch (Baseball)
wild type (Genetics)
[Hyphenate as adj.]
Wild West show
will-call (n., adj.)
willful and wanton
will-less
will-o'-the-wisp
willowware
willpower
willy-nilly
windage
windbag
wind-bell
windblast
windblown
windborne
windbound (Nautical)
windbreak
Windbreaker™
wind-broken (of horses)
windburn
windchill factor
wind chimes
wind cone
wind-down
wind erosion
windfall
wind gauge
windjammer
windmill
window box
window dresser
window dressing
windowpane
window seat
window shade
window-shop (v.)
windowsill
windpipe
wind-pollinated
wind power

windproof
wind scale
wind-screen
wind shake
wind-shaken
wind shear
windshield wiper
windsock
wind sprint
windstorm
windsurf (v.)
Windsurfer™
windsurfing
windswept
windtight
wind tunnel
windup (n.)
windward
Windy City (Chicago)
wine cellar
wine cooler
wineglass
winegrower/winegrowing
winemaker/winemaking
winepress
wineskin
winetaster/winetasting
wing and wing (Nautical)
wingback (Football)
wing chair
wing collar
wing dam
wingding
wing flat (Theater)
wing-footed
wingman (Aeronautics)
wing nut
wingover (Aeronautics)
wingspan
wingspread
wing tip
winner's circle

winning opening (Tennis)
winterfeed (v., n.)
winter garden
winter-hardy
winterkill (v., n.)
win-win (adj.)
wiped-out (adj.)
wipeout (n.)
wire brush (n.)
wire-brush (v.)
wire cloth
wire cutter
wiredraw (v.)
wiredrawn
wirehaired
wire house (Stock Exchange)
Wirephoto™ (n., v.)
wirepuller/wirepulling
wire recording
wire service
wiresonde (Meteorology)
wirespun
wire-stitch (Bookbinding)
wiretap (n., v., adj.)
wiretapper
wire transfer (n.)
wire-transfer (v.)
wireway
wirework(s)
wire-wound resistor
    (Electricity)
wiseacre
wiseass (adj., n.)
wisecrack
wise guy (n., adj.)
wise man
wisenheimer
wishbone
wishful thinking
wish list
wish-wash: Foolish writing;
    watery soup.

wishy-washy
witchcraft
witch doctor
witches' brew
witch hazel
witch-hunt (n., v.)
witch-hunting
witching hour
withdrawal syndrome
withindoors
within-named
with-it (adj.)
withoutdoors
witness box
witness protection
  program
witness stand
woebegone
wolf call
wolf-child
wolf pack
woman about town
woman-chaser
woman-day
womanhater
womanhood
woman-hour
woman in the street:
  Respectable citizen.
womanizer
woman of letters
woman of the streets:
  Prostitute.
woman of the world
womanpower
woman suffrage
woman-year
womb-to-tomb (adj.)
womenfolk
womenkind
women's liberation
women's rights

women's wear
wonder boy/wonder child
wonder drug
wonderland
wonder-stricken
wonderwork/
  wonderworker
won ton (Chinese cookery)
woodbin
woodblock (n., adj.)
woodborer/woodboring
woodcarver/woodcarving
woodchopper
woodcraft/woodcrafter
woodcraftsman
woodcut/woodcutter
woodenhead
woodenheaded
wooden Indian
wooden shoe
woodenware
woodgrain
woodlander
woodman
wood nymph
woodpile
wood pitch
woodprint
wood pulp
wood screw
woodshed
wood shot (Tennis, etc.)
wood tar
woodturner/woodturning
woodwind (Music)
woodwork/woodworker/
  woodworking
woolgather (v.)
woolgathering (n.)
woolgrower
woolly-headed
word association test

word-blind (adj.)
word blindness
wordbook
word deafness
word for word
word game
wordlore
wordmonger/
  wordmongering
word of honor
word of mouth
word order
word painting/
  word picture
wordplay
word processing/
  word processor
wordsmith
word stress
word time (Computers)
word wrap
workaday (adj.)
workaholic/workaholism
workbasket
workbench
workboat
workbook
work camp
workday
worked-up (adj.)
workers' compensation
work ethic
workfare
work farm
workflow
work force
workhorse
work-hour
workhouse
working capital
working class [Hyphenate
  as adj.]

working day [Hyphenate as
  adj.]
working girl
working hour
workingman/
  workingwoman
working order
working papers
working storage
  (Computers)
workload
workman
workmanlike
workmanship
work of art
work order
workout
workpiece
workplace
workprint (Movies)
work-release
workroom
work rules
work sheet
workshop
workspace
workstation
work stoppage
work-study program
worktable
workup
workweek
World Bank
worldbeater
world-class (adj.)
World Court
World Cup (Soccer)
worldly-minded
worldly-wise
world power
world premiere
world's fair

worldshaker/worldshaking
world-view: Translation of German *Weltanschauung*.
world war
world-weary
worldwide
worm drive (Machinery)
worm-eaten
worm gear
wormhole
worm's-eye view
wormwood
worn-out
worry beads
worrywart
worst-case (adj.)
would-be (adj.)
wrack and ruin: Rack and ruin.
wraparound (n., adj.)
wraparound mortgage
wrap-up
wrecker's ball
wrecking car (Railroad)
wrecking crane
wrigglework
wristband
wristlock (Wrestling)
write-down (Accounting)
write-in (n., adj.)
write-off
writer's block
writer's cramp
write-up
writ of certiorari (Law)
writ of error (Law)
wrongdoer/wrongdoing
wrongful death
wrongheaded
wrong number
wrought-up (adj.)
wry-necked

wunderkind (G.; pl. **wunderkinder**): Child prodigy.

X

x-axis (Mathematics)
X chromosome
xenograft (Surgery)
xenophile/xenophilia
xenophobe/xenophobia
xerography
Xerox™
X-linked (Genetics)
X-rated
NOTE: X ray, X-ray, x ray, x-ray? Dictionaries differ. Says the *American Heritage*, "**x-ray** (n.) Also, **x ray, X ray, X-ray.**" Of the six dictionaries checked (two of them medical), four go with the lowercase hyphenated **x-ray** for both noun and verb, as set forth below.
x-ray (n.)
x-ray (v.)
x-ray plate/x-ray print
x-ray technician
x-ray therapy

Y

yacht club
yachtsman/yachtsmanship
yachtswoman
yahoo
yakety-yak (v.)
yakety-yakking (n.)

183

y'all: You all.
yardarm
yardbird
yard goods
yardman
yardmaster
yard sale
yardstick
yard work
yarmulke
yarn-dyed
year-around (adj.): Year-round.
yearbook
year-end
yearlong
year-round (adj.)
year-rounder
yeasayer
yeast cake
yellow alert
yellow-bellied (adj.)
yellowbelly (n.): A coward.
yellowcake
yellow dog
yellow-dog contract
yellow fever
yellow flag (quarantine)
Yellow Pages
yeoman of the guard
yes-man
yes-no question
yes-or-no answer
yesteryear
yin and yang
yo-heave-ho
yokefellow
Yom Kippur
yoo-hoo
you-all: You, Southern style.
young blood (n.)
young-blood (adj.)

young-eyed
Young Turk
yours truly
you-uns: Southern.
yo-yo (n., adj., v.)
yum-yum

Z

Zeitgeist (G.): Spirit of the time.
zero-base
zero-based
zero-coupon (adj.)
zero gravity
zero hour
zero population growth
zero-sum (adj.)
zigzag
zip code (n.)
zip-code (v.)
zip gun
zip-in (adj.)
Ziploc™
zip-out (adj.)
zoom lens